Finish Big With No Regrets

How to Sell Your Mid-Sized Business

Second in a Woodbridge International series.
The first book "How to Sell Your Mid-Sized Business"
was published in early 2018.

"How to Sell Your Mid-Size Business" can be downloaded
free on our website and is available in hard-copy and as an audiobook.

www.woodbridgegrp.com

Contact one of our Business Development experts.
Call 203-389-8400

Greg Michaels: ext. 210 | gmichaels@woodbridgegrp.com
Don Krier: ext. 201 | dkrier@woodbridgegrp.com
Larry Reinharz: ext. 209 | lreinharz@woodbridgegrp.com

By Gus Venditto/Lori Green, Editor

ISBN: 978-0-578-43740-8

Legal Disclaimers and End User Rights

First Printing

Table of Contents

Introduction: You're Ready to Sell Your Business: How Do You Finish Big with No Regrets?

This book is for business owners who are ready to sell their business and finish big with no regrets. If you want to achieve the best results for you, your family and your team, you can't rely on the way selling a business has always been done.

The close rate for businesses sold in the middle-market by traditional M&A firms is about 30%. Woodbridge has a close rate north of 80%. How do you make sure that your business is one of those that actually sells? There is a simple solution: You go to more buyers and get more bids at higher prices from buyers who are a better fit. That's the way to sell your business, finish big and have no regrets. But you need a proven methodology and a team of people that are obsessed with making this happen.

To do what is right for you, your employees, and the people who helped get you there, you need to start with the end in mind. By setting the closing date, or drop-dead date, upfront and having confidence that you will have multiple bidders, it will ensure that your dreams will come true.

In this book, you will learn how to make this happen.

Consider these two different stories with very different outcomes.

A traditional M&A firm took a company in the herbal products business to market. They went to about 150 buyers and let these buyers know that if they were willing to pay a 5x multiple for the business, they could buy it. That's the traditional way. After one unfunded sponsor agreed to the price, the company was taken off the market, and the deal was closed.

Consequently, the owner of the herbal business was not given any choice. There was only one buyer and that buyer was not properly vetted. The new buyer said the owner could stay on for two years and be treated as a partner. But the buyers were wolves in sheep's clothing. They were not who they said they were.

The company had been run by a husband and wife who were deeply passionate about this pristine, growing company. The employees were treated like family. Protecting the culture was paramount. And they wanted to produce the highest quality products so consumers could taste the difference. The new owners cared only about cutting overhead and bringing in more revenue.

As part of the deal, there was a 20% rollover of equity and a note with 8% interest that was to be paid over five years. After six months of pure hell, the new buyers forced the former owners out of the business. The new owners thought they knew better and did not want to listen.

After a year and a half, the new owners did an add-on acquisition of a business with $2 million in EBITDA and folded it into the business. As part of the funding for the add-on acquisition, the former owners had the opportunity to cash out their 20% ownership.

However, one year later, the company is about to go into bankruptcy with two years of principal left on the note. Many key employees left, and the remaining employees are not motivated. The culture is gone and sales are declining.

The moral of the story: Because there was only one buyer, the owner was left with deep regrets about selling it. We believe when you have one buyer, you have no buyers. Sellers need choice.

Another example is a service business with three owners. In this case, Woodbridge marketed the company to more than 15,000 strategic and financial buyers selected from our database of 350,000 active buyers. Out of those contacts, 239 potential buyers signed a confidentiality agreement and received a book and video about the company.

From the 239 potential buyers, we received 43 bids, and the top 10 bidders came in for management meetings. Our client wanted a 6x multiple – but we got them a 13x multiple from a private equity group with $60 billion under management. The private equity group saw this acquisition as a great fit with another company in their portfolio. They paid the 13x because they saw the intense competition for the company. They saw the future of this company and the synergy with their portfolio company. And they were excited to bring on the three owners to continue with the company.

We went to market with big, bold thinking as we always do. We had no asking price. Our clients did better than they expected and they are excited about the future. They finished big and have no regrets.

Taking the Next Step Toward Your Best Outcome

You have taken your business as far as you've dreamed and now it's time for someone else to carry the torch. Your best outcome is to sell for the most amount of money, leave your company in good hands and have no regrets. We understand this.

You are no doubt looking for this process to create a significant return for you and to preserve your legacy. You've invested years of hard work in your business and it's time to cash in. You've created a significant amount of value. You have every right to transform your life and find the best buyer.

At Woodbridge International, we have worked with thousands of business owners like yourself who have built solid businesses and moved on to the next stage in their lives. We understand what business owners are looking for: a great outcome for themselves, their colleagues and their company. We understand you. Our world revolves around you. We are in business to positively transform your life. And we care. You are the reason Woodbridge exists.

We want you to finish big and have no regrets.

To achieve this, we assembled a passionate, fanatical team of subject matter experts. They are the best at what they do: researching, marketing, closing and managing the process. And they all understand that the closing date is a deadline just like a wedding date. You will learn that there is only one best way to do this: The Woodbridge Way.

Woodbridge is committed to helping our clients achieve a positive transformation in their lives. Positively transforming the lives of business owners is our only business.

Selling a business is life-changing for the owner. It means having financial freedom and the opportunity to have new choices in life. We hear clients say they want to travel and have some time to recharge themselves. It may mean spending more time at a hobby or starting one. It may even mean staying on in the business and rewriting your job description so that you spend more time doing what you love doing and less time doing things you don't enjoy doing. The post-sale transformation leads to new opportunities and a new outlook on life.

We approach the process as a partnership. We believe that when we do our job well, we are helping business owners achieve their goals and lifelong dreams. We are providing our clients with choice. We know that when you have only one buyer, you really have no choice. With one buyer, you will only have regrets because you have not truly tested the market and selected the best fit. You need contrast among buyers so you can choose.

The Woodbridge team is prepared to fight for you and obtain every dollar. Our process is engineered to fight for every opportunity to raise the value of your company and close as fast as possible, which is in your best interest.

To create the best deal possible, we are prepared to be unreasonable during negotiations.

We want you to close with the right buyer: one who sees what you see and is ready to take your company into the future.

Since 1993, we have positively transformed more business owners' lives than anyone else we know. And we continue to close more deals every year in every imaginable industry niche. We've seen it all: the great and the perfect deals. And we've seen why deals blow up. You need to imagine your journey with us is like riding the perfect wave, which means closing a deal in 150 days where together we are completely in control of the timing.

As you might imagine, the team has witnessed a wide range of deals that involved all types of buyers and sellers. The members of the team are continually sharing what they've learned in an effort to help our clients achieve their dream of finishing big with no regrets. To ensure you sell for the most amount of money to the buyer with the best fit, we set a drop-dead closing date. You'll be sure your deal will close on the closing date because we work to a timeline and keep everyone accountable and on track.

Our process includes a 2-day workshop where you participate with other business owners to learn what it takes to sell your business to the best buyer, with the best fit and for the most money. Here you will learn how to think like a buyer and how to raise the value of your company. As far as we know we are the only M&A firm offering this.

We believe Woodbridge International is like a university and you are getting the highest level of education and insight from our never-ending crusade to find the best way forward for you. We are constantly challenging the status quo and teaching based on what we've learned.

The reason we have created *Finish Big With No Regrets: How to Sell Your Mid-Sized Business* is because we have observed that too many business owners take this momentous step without understanding that they need to have multiple bidders. You want a buyer to buy in to your company's purpose and to be able to grow the company to the next level. You want to pick the buyer who understands that your business is a collection of all of your people and not just you.

The details of selling a mid-size company have been cloaked in mystery, and the large M&A firms and industry-specific brokers like it that way. It helps them to hide why they get their mediocre results (or no results – few bids or no bids). They believe it's all about who they know and their individual skill set instead of a novel, proven, time-tested team approach.

They think the fewer buyers you go to, the more you'll get. We think that with big, bold thinking you get big, bold results. We know that going to more buyers gets you more bids. Competition not only educates you about what the market will pay, more importantly, it gives you more options so you can select the best fit.

We believe in putting the odds in your favor and betting on every horse.

The big M&A firms and industry boutiques want to do deals with people they have done deals with before because it's easier. They are not there to educate you. It's easier for the investment banker to put you at a disadvantage because they just want to get a deal done as quickly as possible at any cost and get on to the next one. They don't care what happens after the sale. They don't understand that you have to be able to pick and choose by comparing one buyer to another, so you will be able to finish big with no regrets because there is competition.

We are different. We want to give you a fighting chance to sell your company to someone who wants to build on what you've created. We've got your back. We want to give you insight into how buyers think so you can pick the best one among them.

You're going to learn what to say and how to engage buyers. We'll help you improve what you will get for your business. You'll learn the secrets that other M&A firms don't want you to know. We're leveling the playing field and giving you an advantage because knowledge is power.

We work with our clients to educate them on every step of the process so they'll be in a position to obtain the best results possible. And we've embraced the changes that have been made possible by improving the way M&A is done.

"Today's technology allows access to information like no other time in history," said Don Krier, Partner and Managing Director at Woodbridge, in the book *How to Sell Your Mid-Size Business*. "Traditional M&A firms still think going to less will get you more – they still think it's all about relationships and who you know. But their way will not get you the best results."

The Woodbridge database contains hundreds of thousands of potential buyers of mid-size companies. So we can market your business to thousands of strategic buyers and PE groups that have the means and desire to buy a company like yours.

Why do it the old way when new thinking, marketing and technology is available to improve the way it can be done?

We've created this book as another step toward educating our clients so they can reach their goals and transform to what's next. It contains the lessons we've learned through more than 25 years of helping business owners transform their lives.

We hope you'll use this book at the beginning of the sales process to educate yourself and then come back to it along the way, as you work to create the best possible outcome for you and your company.

"When you think about selling your business, think about it like you're telling a story to the marketplace," advises Bryan Wallace, Director at Woodbridge. "The story of your company will have ups and downs. There will be threats and there will be opportunities for your company in the story. However, the most important part of your story is where it's going and who will take it there."

We want you to tell the story of why you built your business. It's a story that goes far beyond your current EBITDA. We want you to tell buyers why your company exists, what the future story is, and who will carry the torch. What single thing does your company do better than anyone else in the world? Help buyers understand the full value of your company and the people that you surround yourself with.

In the following chapters, we will share how we create a compelling story. You'll understand the must-haves for a buyer. And how to close a deal that can give you the best possible outcome for you, your company, your colleagues and your family.

We are thrilled to be your partner in this exciting journey. We know what matters to you, and we will help you achieve it.

Chapter 1: Learning the Perspective of a Buyer

There is a common theme in the deals that create maximum value for the seller, and it is fairly simple: The best deals are made when the seller presents a company that meets or exceeds the buyer's expectations. It sounds obvious, doesn't it? But the reality is that most business owners aren't thinking about their businesses this way.

It's understandable. As a business owner, you are 100% focused on growing your company. You have become an expert in your company's operations and in your industry.

Now that you are preparing to sell your company, it's time to take on a new priority: preparing your company for its next owner.

Even if you are just starting to prepare your business for a sale, it is not too early to start thinking about how potential buyers will look at your company. The day will come all too soon when you will be face-to-face with the people who are interested in buying your company. Preparation for these meetings will take time and careful thought. And, unlike any other M&A firms, we prepare you for this day with extensive training.

> "We have sold companies for 4x recast EBITDA up through 15x EBITDA, for 50% of revenue and 400% of revenue. And others we've sold simply for the asset value. While the history of the company is important, where the company is positioned to go into the future is even more important. Because buyers are buying the future."
>
> *Don Krier*
> *Partner and Managing Director*
> *Woodbridge International*

When you are face-to-face with potential buyers, they will be very polite in acknowledging the great work you've done in building your company. But the buyer will be more concerned with the answer to this question: "If I do this deal, will I see a substantial return on my investment?"

How you answer that question will determine whether you have a deal or not. And it will play a significant role in the price you get.

Buyers are not just buying a company, they are buying the team that got you here. The buyer wants to feel confident that they will get a team that can take this company to the next level and increase its value and market position.

A buyer will not go through the considerable amount of work and commitment of capital only to continue your business at its current level of profitability or revenue. Buyers are usually looking for a long-term return of 2.5x – 3x their investment, or a 20% IRR (Internal Rate of Return).

That doesn't mean the buyers have unreasonable growth expectations. They might bring additional resources to add on to your business. They may currently own or have plans to acquire related businesses that have synergies with your business. And they may own technologies or business platforms that can accelerate revenue growth when integrated with the current operation. The buyer wants proof that the business is sustainable beyond where you are today. The buyers will look to your people – 60% of their decision will be based on your people and what their role will be post-closing.

However, bear in mind, you will have limited control, if any, over what the buyer does after the sale. That's why you need multiple buyers, so you have insight into how the various buyers would run your business after the sale. Before the sale, how you and your team tell the story of your company and its potential will have a significant impact on the value you receive.

Convincing the Buyer You Will Provide a Smooth Transition

Buyers will need to be convinced that your business can operate without your direct involvement after the sale so that a smooth transition can take place with minimal disruption. To achieve the best possible deal, you need to be able to engage the buyer in what makes your company tick. And they need to understand who is helping you achieve it. Be ready to tell a story about your company that will convince the buyer that there will be no unpleasant surprises after the deal is closed.

> The more a buyer buys into your company's purpose and your people, the less regret you will have.

Being able to express why the company exists is critical. Can you express your purpose in a few words? What is your core ideology? What is your "why"? Why do you do what you do?

Companies do better when people from within are promoted, as Jim Collins wrote in *Built to Last*. The more your company is a turnkey operation, the less the buyer has to do and the more likely it will be acquired. Can you identify who is going to carry the torch into the future? Who is aligned with you, your vision, purpose and priorities? Who can do things better than you do?

Buyers want to build on what you've created without a lot of risk - and get a return on their money. How predictable have you made your business? Do you and your people think big? Are you moving your business forward and achieving key performance results? A buyer wants to buy where your company is going. The clearer you are about future opportunities, the better your chance of obtaining a premium price. Identify your biggest contributors and give them a voice.

None of us is as smart as all of us. And buyers understand this.

A common mistake made by entrepreneurs is to enter into the sales process with a self-centered view of their business. It's understandable why this happens. For years, the leader of a company gets his or her identity from the company. It becomes their alter ego. The more they pour themselves into it, the more it becomes a part of them. However when you are selling your company, you're selling where it's going. If you will no longer be part of it, buyers must be convinced that your people can carry on without you.

You have every right to be proud of the work you've done in building your business. But can your company carry on without you? Otherwise you may have nothing to sell.

It is essential that the buyer gains confidence that the business will thrive even if you (and your partners) are no longer actively involved. That's an important consideration even if you are open to staying on with new owners. You need to look out the window and attribute success to factors other than yourself. You need to set up your successors for even greater success.

This is not the time to emphasize how important your contributions have been. This is a time to think about how self-sufficient your company will be with the team that you have attracted and trained.

Business author Jim Collins summarizes the attributes of great leaders as those who "display a powerful mixture of personal humility and indomitable will. They're incredibly ambitious, but their ambition is first and foremost for the cause, for the organization and its purpose, not themselves."

Many entrepreneurs enter the sales process with the expectation that they can sell the company without telling their senior management team about the plan. This can be a fatal mistake. Buyers will need to be assured that operations can continue under their ownership.

The idea of buying a turnkey business is very reassuring to buyers. They will always insist on meeting the managers who will stay on after the sale. It is not a good idea to wait until the last moment to bring your top managers into the sales process. In Chapter 5, we'll discuss the strategies that can guide you through this process.

Preparing for Strategic and Financial Buyers

The best deals are made when multiple parties bid on a company, creating competition among potential acquirers. To give you the most options and obtain the best possible deal, you will want to attract bids from both strategic buyers and financial buyers.

A strategic buyer is a company that sees synergy between your operations and its own. It may be a competitor or operate in a related field. A strategic buyer might have an existing management structure that may be ready to take over your operations and fold it into its own organization. But in most cases, a strategic buyer may not be in a position to do that. They will need to be assured that your management team is prepared to continue without disruption.

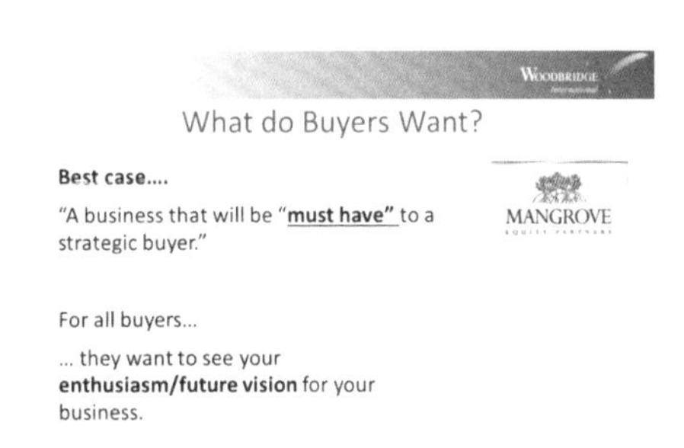

Financial buyers include private equity groups and family funds. A private equity group will look at your company solely as an investment that they will sell for a profit at a later date. They are interested in buying companies that are capable of operating and growing independently. They may have a portfolio company that will have a strategic interest in your company, but they still will be relying on your people to carry on. Family funds may want to hold onto business indefinitely.

One of your goals should be to create a story about your company that can work for either a strategic or a financial buyer. In Chapter 4, we will look closely at the issues you'll need to address in preparing your current management team for discussions with various types of potential buyers.

This is not to say that your managers will take over the process of selling your company and you have a passive role. Far from it. Your active involvement is essential. You need to be a passionate advocate for the future of your company. You and your team need to express excitement about your company and infect others with enthusiasm for the future of your company. The buyer won't give you a do-over. You need to be ready to present your company with energy and commitment.

"If you and your team can't see the future for your business, why would a buyer?" said Bryan Wallace, Director, Woodbridge International, in a workshop on how to prepare for meetings with potential buyers.

In Chapter 2, we'll look closely at our marketing process. You'll learn how each step is managed by experts to maximize your company's value and provide you with the best choice of buyers so you can finish big and have no regrets.

Chapter 2: The Woodbridge Deal Process: Generating Options

With over 25 years of success in selling mid-sized companies, Woodbridge has developed a system that can create the right conditions for a seller to obtain maximum value for their company. When a seller signs on with Woodbridge, they take on a partner who brings a team of experts with years of experience in selling mid-size companies.

Each member of the Woodbridge team knows exactly how to execute and complete their tasks in a timely manner - otherwise time will kill your deal.

The Woodbridge team performs all the essential tasks required for a successful sale. It will produce a book, known as the Confidential Information Memorandum (CIM), that tells your story in a compelling way, with an emphasis on your future story. Woodbridge's underwriters will dig into your financial statements, prepare a compelling financial presentation and uncover potential issues in your business that may surprise buyers.

And it will prepare a comprehensive marketing campaign to generate as many bids as possible from buyers that are interested in acquiring companies like yours.

The marketing campaign is one of the biggest differences between Woodbridge and other M&A firms. That's how you will go through the process, finish big and have no regrets. More buyers, more bids, higher price, better fit.

At the beginning of the process, the Woodbridge team prepares a comprehensive marketing campaign that is unique in the M&A industry. The marketing campaign includes a professionally written descriptive memorandum explaining your company's operations, financial statements, and a video that showcases your business. We have our own 350,000-name database of strategic buyers to use. Each campaign will be targeted to 7,000-10,000 strategic companies and related buyers plus 4,500 private equity groups.

Typically, 150 of those buyers will sign confidentiality agreements and receive the book and video. Our competitors - who approach only 50 to 200 buyers - can't achieve this because they want to market to a small, select group of buyers and rely on their relationships. However, we know there are always thousands of potential buyers for a mid-size company. No one can accurately pre-select a few and be confident they have included all the best buyers.

We then solicit bids. It's from those bids, an average of 15, that we choose the most enthusiastic buyers who desire (and have the resources) to do the deal and own your company. We know no one else can deliver this number of bids. This is a game changer. You are in a position to decide on the best buyer for your business vs. having only one buyer. Or, no buyers.

We learn their reasons for bidding before we meet with them, so we can tailor the meeting for them. If you know what the buyer is thinking prior to the meeting you will be in the best position to make a choice.

At the heart of the Woodbridge process is the 150-day timeline, which is established for every company we take to market. It documents deadlines for all of the essential tasks. One of the innovations that has made Woodbridge so successful in the M&A world is the concept of starting with a "predefined drop-dead closing date." It becomes like a wedding date: You just don't miss it because it's the beginning of your new life.

Delays always work in the favor of the buyer.

Most M&A firms leave the closing date open-ended and, as a result, getting your deal closed is nothing more than a dream and not a goal because goals are dreams with deadlines. Woodbridge clients can attest that one reason why the company is so successful in closing deals is because Woodbridge team members, our clients and attorneys are focused on keeping to that drop-dead timeline.

"They were always ready to do what needed to be done to get my business sold for the highest possible price for my company and find the best buyer," said Jim Polley, CEO of Vanguard Dealer Services.

Polley had thought about selling the company himself but came to realize, as he put it, "It's a pretty big world out there with a lot of different possibilities." And when Woodbridge obtained 40 bids for his company, he knew he had made the right decision. Polley had never heard of the acquiring company, a private equity firm. **In fact, 75% of the time we sell to a buyer our client didn't know.**

Creating a Sense of Urgency

One of the most important lessons Woodbridge has learned is the need to create a sense of urgency during the sales process. In the 150-day Woodbridge timeline, every day matters. Delay is never to the advantage of the seller. In fact, time kills deals.

Buyers will always find reasons to delay, hoping to have more time to observe the performance of your company over a longer period. If something bad were to happen it would give the buyer the opportunity to lower the price and re-trade the deal. We can't let this happen. Here are some of the real-life Buyer Delay Tactics we've run into and the best practices we use to counter them:

- Vacations. Mitigate by making sure no one takes vacations from LOI to Closing.
- Sympathy. Never take the pressure off; drive to get the deal closed on the closing date.
- Customer surveys. Woodbridge does customer surveys so we are not caught off guard if we allow the buyer to do it.
- Due diligence. Have the data room 100% complete; track progress.
- Never-ending questions. At some point the buyer needs to be told that it just doesn't matter: We are closing on the closing date or we are done. And moving to the next group of buyers waiting in the wings.

- Putting doubt in everyone's mind about the future. Present and maintain throughout the process that the future is bright and they close on the closing date or they're done.
- Quality of Earnings report. Woodbridge produces a Quality of Earnings analysis that is the baseline.
- Running the closing process in series. The buyer is acting as if they will find something in due diligence that will make them decide not to do the deal or do the deal at a lower price. Woodbridge did the underwriting and we know the company is bulletproof so there will be no reason the diligence will lead to a re-trade. That's why we have the legal documents produced at the same time as due diligence is being done...so the deal closes on the closing date.
- The buyer's attorney creates obstacles. Weekly all-hands calls checking how everyone is doing against the checklist and the timeline.
- Taking time to draft the LOI. Woodbridge has an LOI template for buyers to use.
- No actual closing date agreed to in LOI. LOI should have an agreed-upon closing date with consequences.

Unforeseen circumstances can create unfavorable market conditions. Deadlines are the best way to elicit competitive bids from multiple parties. We build deal momentum because deal drag is a disaster. That's why we always start with the end date in mind.

Time Kills Deals

Time kills deals. Entrepreneurs who have sold their companies with Woodbridge come to understand the wisdom of this phrase.

The process of bringing a company to market requires careful preparation. Underwriters need to review and vet financial statements and business operations. Marketers are your biggest advocate to get buyers to put forth bids; they create a compelling story about your company. And all the potential acquirers need to be contacted. The process will build deal momentum and tension, leading to a competitive bidding process.

But each one of these steps introduces the potential for delay and indecision. When delay sets in, obstacles can emerge that threaten a deal. Market conditions may deteriorate. Your company may lose key clients. And potential buyers may become distracted by other opportunities.

"All it takes is a hurricane, a crucial employee with a sudden health issue, a product issue or a lawsuit to sabotage the momentum of a sale process that is moving in the right direction," explains Andrew Buchholtz, Woodbridge Partner and Managing Director.

To ensure you as the seller have every advantage, you need to stay focused on your 150-day timeline with the goal of a closing on the drop-dead closing date. The schedule creates a sense of urgency around the deal. Potential buyers know that you are serious about making a deal and that other parties will be given the same chance to review the company and make a bid.

Companies that acquire businesses are familiar with the process of a deadline; it helps them prioritize their own schedule. Their internal analysts and lawyers will be able to adjust their schedules so that they have enough time to take a close look and to move quickly. By establishing a closing date at the very beginning of the process, Woodbridge is setting the table for a competitive bidding process, the best way to obtain maximum value.

"It was highly important to have a pre-set closing date," said Ryan Ermeling, founder of Stretch Internet, who said the Woodbridge process helped him obtain a price that was significantly higher than he had anticipated. "I went into the process with a number that I would have been very happy with and we ended with a number that was 50% higher than that."

Confidential Auction in 150 Days	
• Service Agreement Signed	Day 0
• Kick-off Meeting P&S Agreement Draft	Day 5
• Information for Marketing Material Provided	Day 12
• Client Financial Information Provided	Day 12
• Global Marketing List Finalized	Day 33 Day
• Draft Memorandum to Client	33
• Video to Client	Day 35
• Financial Draft Completed and sent to Client	Day 38
• Client Sign-off on Financials and Video	Day 40
• Draft 1-Pager to Client	Day 41
• Client Sign-off on Memorandum & 1-Pager	Day 42
• Market launch	Day 45
• Data Room Complete	Day 45
• 2-Day Management Meeting Workshop	Day 50
• P&S Agreement Complete/Add to Dataroom	Day 60
• 21 Day Bid Acceptance Period Closes	Day 66
• Management Meetings Complete	Day 87
• LOI's Received	Day 94
• LOI's Signed (Pre-Negotiated fixed Legal Fee applied)	Day 101
• Drop-Dead Date (Closing Deadline)	Day 150

Moving quickly does not mean cutting corners. The Woodbridge timeline provides adequate time to create a marketing campaign for each client that will impress potential acquirers and elicit multiple bids. We follow the schedule closely, and it works best when you are on board.

Starting on the day a seller signs an agreement with Woodbridge, the clock starts ticking. On day 5, a kick-off conference call takes place. Attending this call is the research team and your deal closer, an experienced M&A professional who will advise you throughout the process. The closer will help you decide who to bring to management meetings and coach you and your team on how to present. The closer will practice with you, guide you through the management meetings, negotiate the letters of intent, and then remove every obstacle to get the deal closed on the closing date deadline.

Ryan Ermeling said that he chose Woodbridge after comparing it to an industry-specific firm. "The M&A firm that specialized in technology that I was speaking with said they were only going to reach out to 60 to 80 companies that they felt good about," he explained. He went with Woodbridge after learning that they would approach more than 15,000 strategic buyers and private equity groups.

You need to provide the background information needed for the marketing campaign, and approvals are needed along the way. Woodbridge provides a questionnaire that will elicit the necessary information. You will be assigned a highly experienced writer from our team of writers who have written hundreds of Confidential Information Memorandums.

A video is created to bring the company to life and to amplify the story told in the written materials.

"The marketing package was so impressive," said Jim Polley. "I was impressed looking at my own company."

Quality of Earnings Analysis

At the same time the marketing package is being created, Woodbridge underwriters are working on creating a Quality of Earnings analysis that provides a credible review of your company's finances in a format buyers want to see.

"Having accurate and timely financial statements is crucial in getting a deal done for maximum value," said Larry Reinharz, Woodbridge Managing Director.

That's why the Woodbridge team of underwriters gets to work on financial statements as soon as the 150-day timeline starts. They aim to complete the underwriting process in the first 30 days but must receive cooperation from you and your accountants. Once again, this is another chance for delay to slow the process down.

Forty days after signing with Woodbridge, the seller will receive a completed book with financial statements and a custom video for review. On day 45, you should have approved the materials so the company can be brought to market. At this point, the Woodbridge marketing department is ready to send emails to buyers selected from our database of 350,000 buyers. The numbers are typically 15,000-25,000 strategic buyers (that make sense) and 4,500 private equity groups.

After buyers sign a confidentiality agreement, they receive the book and video. The bid deadline is 21 days during the marketing phase. We generally invite 5-10 buyers in for management meetings, and only those buyers are given access to the data room.

A complete data room is very important to an efficient deal process. Many deals have gone off the rails when buyers were not able to see the documents they expected. You and our underwriting department will gather the documents and upload them to the data room before the management meetings can begin. That way, everything that needs to be discussed will happen during the management meetings.

Preparing to Meet Potential Buyers

By day 75, all bids should be in. At this point, the seller will stay in close contact with Woodbridge's deal closers to review the bid terms and select the top 5-10 buyers who will be invited to the management meeting. The meeting is usually held at your facility, and buyers will send a small team to meet with the owners and top management.

Chapters 4 and 5 provide in-depth reviews of how Woodbridge helps you take advantage of this opportunity. But first, let's take a look at the bid process and how it works in the next chapter.

Chapter 3: How We Obtain 15 or More Strong Bids for Your Company

After the marketing materials are ready and the target list of potential buyers has been prepared, it is time to take your company to market and solicit bids. This is a critical time in the selling process, and it has been shrouded in mystery by other M&A firms. Woodbridge believes in shedding light on the activities surrounding the sale of mid-size businesses, so let's take a close look at how this process works.

For Woodbridge clients, a marketing campaign begins on Day 45 of the timeline with the goal of having bids in 21 days later – and the marketing doesn't stop until the LOI is signed.

On the day when marketing starts, the following materials are ready to be shared with prospective buyers:

- One-page blind teaser that provides essential facts and highlights about your company is sent to 15,000-25,000 logical, customized strategic and financial buyers.

- Confidentiality agreement, or Non-Disclosure Agreement (NDA), is signed before we send out the CIM and video.

- CIM with the video, often referred to as "the book," to provide detailed information about your company. It includes a brief history of the company, a discussion of the opportunities for growth, a general overview of operations, and basic financial statements with projections for the future.

- Professionally produced video, which is usually two minutes long and includes interviews with the owners and a compelling storyline, gives investors an understanding of the company's success formula.

The marketing campaign gets under way with an outreach to the strategic and financial buyers that have been identified through the research criteria. As discussed in Chapter 2, a list of companies is derived from Woodbridge's proprietary database of 4,500 private equity groups and 350,000 strategic companies. The list is customized with a focus on companies related to your industry that could have an interest in buying your company.

We spend significant time at the kick-off meeting discussing who you think the logical buyers are, and we will approach all of them as well as thousands more.

Our marketers email these companies the one-page teaser. Buyers who express interest are asked to sign an NDA to maintain confidentiality around the process and provide the seller with protection against unnecessary sharing of the materials. Woodbridge marketing associates maintain close contact with potential buyers, offering as much information and support as possible to encourage bids before the deadline.

"The one goal that we share is maximizing the value of your business and getting the deal done as efficiently as possible, because we know you have a business to run," said Bryan Wallace. Once the marketing campaign has started, Woodbridge's marketing team is urged to "push and push and push" to guarantee that all potential buyers are aware that an auction is taking place.

This process creates competitive tension among buyers. They are made aware that other parties are looking at the materials and have the same deadline.

Traditional and industry-focused M&A firms tend to draw out the bid process, doling out materials over a longer period of time, favoring some potential bidders over others in order to preserve their own long-term relationships. This approach allows buyers to take their time and creates very little competitive activity.

The advantage of this broad view of the market can be seen in the success Woodbridge recently had with a client whose business is a membership group for home improvement contractors.

The organization provided information and services to its thousands of members in addition to buying discounts for equipment and supply purchases. Woodbridge prepared materials and went out to market. A major multibillion-dollar private equity firm happened to own a portfolio company in the payment processing business. This payment processing business saw the possibility of capturing the multitude of transactions that the thousands of contractors engaged in through their digital platform.

So they were not just buying the profit of our client's business, they would also generate many times that profit through processing member payments. The synergy they could see between two seemingly unrelated businesses allowed them to justify a stretch and pay 13x EBITDA for the business. No other M&A shop would have marketed as widely and identified and contacted this buyer to begin with. However, once this buyer was identified, our client worked with Woodbridge to build out the story and metrics that would make the brilliance of this deal apparent.

By reaching out to significantly more potential buyers, Woodbridge has had success selling other companies that were considered to be difficult to sell. Here's an example:

Woodbridge was hired by a Midwest website-hosting and server co-location business owned by a delightful man who had built the business and supported his family with it for many years. The business matured and he was able to spend a good amount of time at his home in Florida. The business was no longer growing dramatically, and it faced some large competitors, but he was ready to retire.

After an extensive marketing effort, a strategic buyer emerged who wanted to expand into the seller's region. The transaction went smoothly, and the owner was easily able to transition to a happy retirement, finishing big with no regrets.

Evaluating and Tiering the Bids

After bids are received, it is important to put them in perspective. A bid is far from a final offer. In practical terms, when a bid is made for a company, it is normally presented as a price range. The following table provides a look at the bid process for four recent transactions in different industries.

Industry	Marketing List*	Memorandums	Bids	Bid Range ($M)	Management Meetings	LOI's	Purchase Price ($M)
Healthcare	3,379	140	20	3.6 - 10	9	6	10
Automotive	2,440	184	40	30 - 45	6	5	43
Construction	3,288	164	45	10 - 28	11	9	23
Media	1,529	97	23	22 - 36	13	8	35
* Excluding Private Equity Groups							

The average private equity group operating in the middle market reviews thousands of deal teasers a year. They will sign NDAs and receive the CIM on hundreds of opportunities. After reviewing the materials, they'll attend 10-20 management meetings. And they will ultimately buy only 3-4 companies a year.

The following table shows the deal review schedule at a typical private equity firm. You can see that they received over 22,200 deals over a 7-year period and bought only 24 companies.

2008-2014 Deal Prospecting Statistics

	2008	2009	2010	2011	2012	2013	2014	Aggregate	Avg. Percentage of Deals	Comments
Deals Received	1,224	1,394	1,163	6,518	3,713	3,405	4,813	22,230	100.00%	This figure represents all deals that were received by a typical private equity group.
NDAs Signed	85	261	85	480	159	187	383	1,640	7.38%	This figure represents the number of deals reviewed in detail, which is 7.38% of all deals received.
Broker Calls	45	97	49	115	49	72	106	533	2.40%	This figure represents the number of investment banker phone calls on specific transactions.
IOIs Issued	18	14	11	29	16	16	14	118	0.53%	The private equity group issues an Indication of Interest (IOI) that provides the seller with approximate valuation terms and structure.
Mgt. Visits	11	20	7	26	12	11	11	98	0.44%	Management visits usually consist of an on-site tour of the business and a detailed review of the company's management team.
LOI Submitted	11	10	1	15	11	10	11	69	0.31%	Letters of intent are the formal offers to acquire a company.
LOI Signed	2	6	3	5	6	6	6	34	0.15%	Grand Transformers, Interstate Cleaning Corporation, Vapor Power International, Burgaflex NA, McClarin Plastics, Dickinson Press
Deals Closed, Recaps, Exits*	4	3	2	4	3	3	5	24	0.11%	Platforms: Key Health, Mopec, Grand Transformers, Burgaflex NA, Custom Profile, Staging Concepts Key Health, Amtech

* Not all signed LOIs resulted in a closed deal. Deals are not consummated for the following reasons: (1) business performance changed significantly, or (2) the asset values were determined to be significantly impaired.

The takeaway: a seller must be prepared to meet with multiple bidders in order to obtain the best possible price. And they need to be ready to use those meetings to convince the bidders that the company will be a great investment with as little risk as possible.

The management meetings provide the seller and their team with an opportunity to significantly improve the valuation paid for their company.

Chapter 4: The Management Meeting: Improving the Value of Your Company By Presenting a Defensible Future Story

The most important days in the process of selling your company are the days when you meet with the potential buyers who have expressed interest in acquiring your company by placing a bid. These meetings, which take place around day 87 and last for two weeks of the 150-day timeline, will be your chance to provide the insights and metrics that will convince buyers to submit a higher price in the Letter of Intent (LOI) than they did for the initial bid.

The meetings will be arranged by Woodbridge's staff either at your facility or a nearby hotel. By the time the meeting takes place, these bidders will have already received the materials that Woodbridge created about your company. They will have received written materials that describe your company's operations and provide a brief history. They will have seen financial information and had the opportunity to view a 2-minute marketing video that we created for you.

Buyers will come to this meeting with their own set of assumptions about your company. This is your and your team's opportunity to convince them that your business presents the best possible use of their investment capital and their time. A buyer will come to this meeting after offering a price range for your company and knowing that others have also made bids. We'll invite the top bidders who are most likely to close and have the enthusiasm to buy your business.

The performance you and your team exhibit at these meetings will significantly influence whether those bids go higher, lower or lead to a decision to move forward with a deal.

At this point in the process, the bidding companies have formed an opinion about the business' value based on the marketing package and financial statements they received. And, of course, they performed additional research on their own. So it's safe to say that the bidders have arrived at the conclusion that this is a business they would like to own because they think it presents an opportunity for a significant return on their investment.

But they are depending on the meeting to learn more and help them reach a final decision. They need to have their hopes confirmed and their fears neutralized. The management meetings play a crucial role in moving from bid to LOI. The final value that buyers are willing to pay can change significantly as a result of these meetings.

"Of all the investment banks we considered, Woodbridge had a superior marketing approach. They came up with 6-10 buyers who had a high likelihood of closing the deal, and it became a bidding war. And that's a great position to be in."

-Matt Michel
Former Owner of Service Nation, Inc.

Successful management meetings should lead to an LOI with a price at the high end of the bid range. In some cases, the value goes even higher, thanks to the competitive tension created by having multiple companies involved in the auction.

On the other hand, mistakes at these meetings can result in an offer at the low end of the bid range or, in some cases, no LOI at all.

Woodbridge works with clients to prepare thoughtfully. In the weeks leading up to the management meetings, you need to set aside adequate time to work on a presentation that shows your company at its best. There needs to be new information that will add to the excitement for the buyers.

Woodbridge clients have the advantage of working with an experienced professional who serves as their deal closer. The closer and client work together to create an effective presentation from what they learned in the management meeting workshops. Our closers have a single purpose: identify the best buyer, remove obstacles and get the deal closed. Investment bankers have multiple roles such as generating new clients, writing the offering memorandum, contacting buyers, bringing in a few buyers and attempting to close the deal. They are a jack of all trades and a master of none.

Financial buyers come to management meetings thinking about who the next buyer will be – after them! Their goal is to hold onto the business for a certain period, usually 3-7 years, and then sell it at a profit. Their primary goal at the meeting is to determine if the business confirms their optimistic view of the business' growth potential and how strong the management team is to carry the ball forward.

Financial investors have told investment professionals over and over that one of the primary things they hope to see at a management meeting is enthusiasm from the seller and their team. They want the owners to explain why it is a business worth investing in. To be convinced, they need to see the current owner and managers demonstrate the company has a believable future story.

Creating a Sense of Excitement

Entrepreneurs who have achieved success always bring a passion to the enterprise. The only way to motivate a team of people to build a successful company is to generate vision, purpose, energy and passion. You may not show it every day, but deep down you certainly feel passionately about the company you created.

Now that you have reached the point where you are ready to sell, it's essential that you tap into that passion so buyers can understand the potential you and your team see in the company. That passion can also fuel a sense of urgency about the sales process, creating more enthusiasm from the buyers about the need to own your business. We strongly suggest reading the book *Start with Why: How Great Leaders Inspire Everyone to Take Action* by Simon Sinek.

The Woodbridge process was created to support sellers as they work through the process of selling their company. But it will work best when the seller is able to identify the business' purpose and can share it, making sure everyone in the company is aligned with the purpose and can articulate it.

"Work with us to make the management presentations as strong as possible so that everyone who meets you and sits through the management presentation says, 'I must go into that business, and I'm willing to pay more than I bid initially,' " said Andrew Buchholtz, Woodbridge Managing Director/Partner and Head of Closing.

Mistakes That Can Lower Valuation

At a recent Management Meeting Workshop, Rez Mahboubi, a Woodbridge Vice President who has 25 years of experience in M&A and corporate development, shared the biggest mistakes that he has seen sellers make in management meetings over the years.

- **Lack of enthusiasm**. Buyers often travel long distances to attend these meetings and arrive with great anticipation. They are willing to put their professional reputation on the line to recommend buying your company. And they are looking for managers who are excited about the company they're selling. They can lose interest if the seller does not demonstrate genuine passion for the business and its future story.

- **Lack of clarity about the reasons for selling**. Mahboubi says when sellers can't articulate a clear reason for selling, it "confuses the hell" out of buyers. They prefer to work with motivated sellers who have a clear goal, such as retirement or the desire to start a new business. Or perhaps they desire to sell only a portion of their equity and have a second bite at the apple with a new owner. If the seller isn't willing to share their reasons for selling, it suggests that the deal will have problems. Does the business have a hidden flaw? Is the buyer not serious about selling? Are they planning to launch a competitive business? If the seller wants to stay on, that should be made clear too.

- **Demonstrating a lack of understanding of your growth drivers**. Buyers want to be reassured that the owner is an expert in this industry and can articulate the reasons why the business has been successful. They expect to hear a vision for the company's future growth that can be supported with data. If they don't hear a clear, optimistic story about the industry and the reasons why this company is well-positioned, they may lose their own sense of optimism. They will question if there is a realistic future story and ask if this company was built to last?

To prepare yourself, we highly recommend reading *Built to Last: Successful Habits of Visionary Companies* by Jim Collins, a highly regarded book on business leadership.

Hitting All the Right Notes

When sellers avoid these mistakes and use the management meetings to create a vision of the company as an engine of growth, they are paving a smooth path to closing or even an increase in the valuation.

Woodbridge's team has seen many deals rise in value between the bid and LOI. The common factor in all of those deals were management presentations that stayed focused on telling a growth story about the business and proving that there is a real likelihood that the company has a robust future.

Preparation is essential. You will have a lot riding on the success of this meeting: Don't cheat yourself by failing to prepare. The following is a checklist of items that need to be considered in advance so that they will be handled correctly:

- **Speakers' roles.** A well-run presentation is rehearsed in advance. Each speaker knows which points they will address. As you prepare your presentation, give careful consideration to whether some parts of the story should be told by some of your leadership team members. Owners are often reluctant to involve any employees. In Chapter 5 we'll look at this question in depth to help you understand your options.

- **Address management roles after the sale.** Buyers come to the meeting looking for an understanding of how the business will be run if they close the deal. It is essential that the buyer is assured that the management team that will stay on post-sale is able to execute the growth story. If you are staying on, this is your time to shine. If you are not, be prepared to praise the quality of your leadership team: Their success is your success.

- **Present the growth story.** This is the single most important theme for the meeting. Be prepared to talk about the reasons why the future of this business is bright. Your presentation should include clear metrics that demonstrate why the business has been successful, beyond the financial statements. Don't allow your presentation to be distracted from this theme. The buyer is hoping to learn about a secret sauce. Be prepared to share the recipe.

- **Be prepared to address concerns.** All buyers come to the management meeting with some concerns. You need to be prepared to address and eliminate these concerns. Preparations start during client management training with your closer, and the closer will later discuss any concerns each buyer has prior to holding a management meeting.

Woodbridge's team of closers is ready to provide help to the sellers during this crucial period. They can serve as a sounding board and consultant. You will have the benefit of learning from many years of experience at these meetings. But the commitment to create a great presentation comes from the seller. Only the seller and his or her team has the knowledge and authority to speak about the company with the passion that this process requires.

Chapter 5: Management Meeting Training: Why & What to Expect

One of the advantages of working with Woodbridge International is that we have developed a process that helps business owners understand how to tell that story.

Woodbridge's 2-day Management Meeting Workshop educates sellers on how they can present their companies to their best advantage and start thinking like buyers. The atmosphere creates a *Shark Tank* effect. The advice sellers receive is a distillation of the knowledge that the Woodbridge team has gained from its experience in selling hundreds of mid-size companies and observations at thousands of management meetings.

Sellers who have attended the training have consistently confirmed its value. The training provides you with the chance to practice your presentation and to hear feedback from our closers who have attended hundreds of these meetings. You'll also learn about mistakes that can dampen the interest of a potential buyer and how to avoid making them.

"What I learned is that I was looking at things through the seller's eyes and not through the buyer's eyes," said a Woodbridge client after attending the workshop. "I realized I had a lot of gaps in my past and future story. The professionals helped me to identify some of my gaps and how to address them."

An owner of a specialty manufacturing company said, "It's not about what I think is important for a buyer. It's much more about what Woodbridge knows buyers are looking for and how to be prepared to have the information buyers are looking for."

"This training was the answer to a lot of questions about how to maximize the value of our sale," said the owner of a healthcare facility.

A current client, the owner of a precision manufacturing company, who completed our management meeting training, said, "We have an opportunity in these management meetings to improve our value. We also have an opportunity to decrease it. So it's very important to be prepared and to tell the story of the company going forward so that we can increase the value of the company."

> "One thing I learned is that time kills deals, and we need to have a certain date and not only stick to it but make sure the buyers stick to it."
>
> *- Owner of national consulting firm*

An owner of a company serving the entertainment industry completed our management training workshop and said, "I enjoyed the interactions with the other members. We challenged each other and we related to each other. If you've never sold a company, you need to learn how to do that. At the Woodbridge training we learned a lot about that process and without that, it's just that much harder to sell the company."

There is so much to do when you sell your business. The process is usually intense. Do you really need one more thing to do, to attend management training for 1½ days?

Well, it depends on the outcome you want. Here's what we all want: to sell your business at a price exceeding your expectations. And to find the best fit.

To help you understand why Woodbridge believes that attendance at a management meeting training session is a "must," consider what motivated us to develop the training. Before we offered management meeting training, our closers worked with sellers to prepare for the meetings, starting about one to two weeks before the management meetings were scheduled to start. There was no formal training, just direct conversation.

We had numerous strong buyers. But too often the outcomes were suboptimal. In many cases, strong bids before management meetings became weak LOIs after the meetings. Too often, buyers were reducing their offers by 20% or more. Why was this happening?

Most sellers were selling a business for the first time, and they didn't know what to do in a management meeting. We decided to create a formal training program based not only on our insights over the last 25 years but from interviewing typical buyers of businesses.

Here are some of the insights we've gleaned:

- **Sellers don't have to be perfect, but they need to be humble**. If a seller is arrogant, yet needed in a transition period after the sale, this is a problem to most buyers. The seller needs to show humility in management meetings.

- **Buyers are buying the future, and they need to hear a strong future story.** All too often sellers were talking about the past, not the future.

- **Burden of proof.** If we say something is so about our future story and should add value to the business, we need to prove it is so. In general, if we don't show some proof, the buyer will not give the point any value.

- **Buyers want to see the team.** They are the future. If we tell a buyer we have a great, innovative, high performing, yet humble team, but don't show the team, we fail the burden of proof criterion. This leads to a deep discount in the offer price. There are risks in telling the wrong key employees about the sale too soon. But there is a price to pay if you don't. Do you want to give up 20% of the sale price? It's pay me now (the risk of telling the team) or pay me later (substantially reduced selling price.)

- **Enthusiasm is essential.** If you aren't enthusiastic about the business, why should the buyer be? The buyer won't fill your enthusiasm deficit. Buyers want to see an enthusiastic seller and an enthusiastic team, telling a great future story.

- **Buyers want to manage risk.** In due diligence, you should expect any skeletons in the closet to come out. You are much better off identifying these issues early on and developing a counter strategy and/or explanation for them. In particular, you should be able to talk knowledgeably about your competition. It's another case of pay me now or pay me later. The trouble with "paying later" is that the buyer who finds a skeleton in the closet wonders what they are missing and becomes skeptical. This depresses the selling price.

- **KPIs and OKRs.** Buyers want to know you have a well-running company, a strong base on which they can build. They want to see your dashboard of Key Performance Indicators (KPIs) and be shown how they tie in to your Objectives and Key Results (OKRs).

There are four key purposes for management meeting training:

1. Drill down on the above points, tailoring them to your business
2. Do a gap analysis one month or more before the management meetings to allow you to prepare adequately for answering expected buyer questions
3. Provide you with a safe venue to practice your speaking skills and to practice answering questions on the fly
4. Training with other non-competitive sellers, you get the benefit of their wisdom, as they challenge you on your statements. You learn how to oscillate your mindset between seller and buyer in order see the world more clearly from the buyer's perspective.

During the training, you will have three breakout sessions to work on:

- Your future story
- Your KPIs
- Handling the buyer's sense of risk.

You will practice the brainstorming art of the "pre-mortem," where you assume your business will never sell, figure out a legitimate reason why this might happen, then develop a counter strategy to make sure it not only sells, but sells at a great price.

In ordinary daily conversation, words that convey negativity and pessimism often are part of our vocabulary. In order to convey enthusiasm and optimism, it can be helpful to emphasize words to use during a presentation that will convey a positive outlook. The following table is an example of the exercises that are part of the management meeting training.

Phrases Conveying Enthusiasm & Opportunity

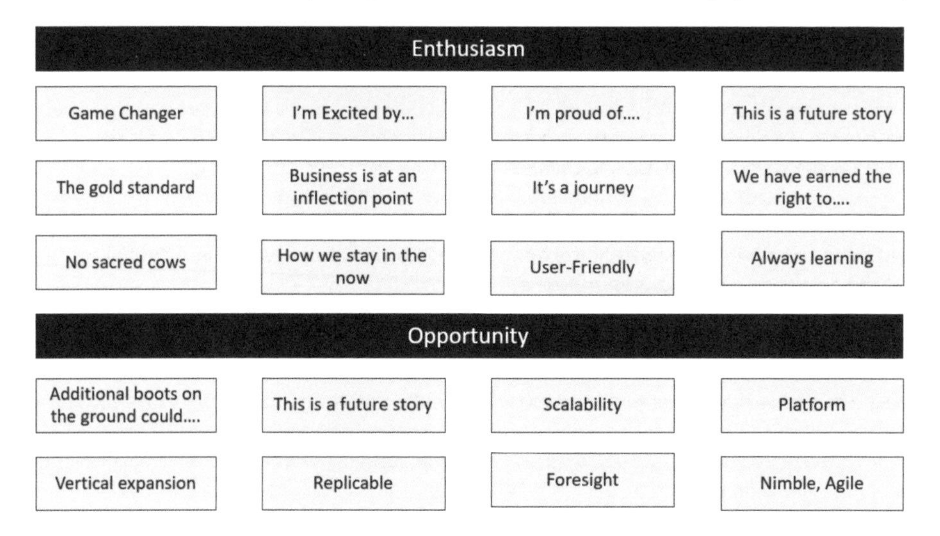

Being Prepared to Listen

Experienced deal closers report that the most successful management meetings are highly interactive with each side talking half the time. So it's important that sellers go into the meetings ready to listen to the buyer's concerns and to answer their questions with explanations for the growth story and the right level of enthusiasm.

"We're going to have to be prepared," said the owner of a lead-generation company after attending a workshop. "We're going to get a lot of questions fired at us that we would not be prepared to answer if we didn't sit down with all of these fellow business owners."

When careful preparation is made before the meeting, not only will the sellers be prepared to make a convincing case, but the Woodbridge closer will be working as a partner to structure the pace of the meeting to give the seller the best chance to make that case.

A management meeting that is properly prepared and executed is a valuable tool in achieving maximum value. It builds the competitive tension that drives buyers to offer an LOI with their best price.

Thinking Like a Buyer

"They trained us to start thinking like a buyer," said a Woodbridge client after attending the Management Meeting Workshop. "Our business is our passion but just because we're thinking one way doesn't mean the buyers are thinking the same way we are."

Another client said he learned at the workshop how important it was to prepare for the questions the sellers would ask and the best way to answer them effectively.

"At the end of the day I am going to be a more effective seller," he said. "I'll be in a better position to convey the strengths of the business and be able to deal with the potential concerns that the buyers are going to present to me."

What does all this mean to you as you select an M&A firm to help sell your business and transition to the next adventure in your life? To ensure you get the right price for your business, select a company that will prepare you to be highly effective during these crucial meetings with buyers.

Chapter 6: Preparing Your Team to Meet the Buyer

If you were going to buy your business, what are the questions you would ask of the owner? And, even more important, who would you want to meet? One of the most significant decisions that the seller of a mid-size company needs to make is who will be the best representative of the company at the management meetings.

Remember, the goal is to create enthusiasm about the future and assure the buyer that the business can continue on after the transaction. When the owners are prepared to stay on and hope to retain a key management role, then of course they should be one of the presenters. But that doesn't mean they should be the only speaker.

One very common way to structure the management meeting is to have the people responsible for different functions speak. The CFO talks about financials. The sales leader talks about customers. Operational leaders explain internal processes. When a team presents the story, buyers will feel more confident about the future. An owner who is not able to comfortably discuss the financial practices or sales relationships will want to bring along someone who can have those conversations at a very detailed level. It is not enough to simply read a prepared statement because the buyers will ask detailed questions.

This is a good time for the owners to take an honest look at their presentation skills. The skills needed to launch and operate a successful business are not necessarily the same skills required to sell the business. In the weeks leading up to the management meetings, the owners should honestly assess the challenge of how to best present the company to buyers.

What Are the Buyer's "Must-Haves"?

Ash Savani, Woodbridge Vice President, recently told a group of sellers at a Management Meeting Workshop that "when everything is done well, the management team is showcased, the growth story is discussed and metrics are presented, it translated into a very positive outcome, most of the people who came to the meetings gave us an LOI."

And in a recent transaction where the selling team hit all of those notes in each of the management meetings, Savani said that multiple companies submitted LOIs and the price went up after the meetings. The seller achieved 50% above their expectation.

A failure to create a positive outlook and stay on script during the meetings can send a company's valuation south.

Tex Sekhon, Woodbridge Senior Vice President, recently took a company to market and received bids in the range of $12.5-$14 million. He said, "The company had a product that was near perfect, but the management meetings did not go as well as they could."

One of the two partners was quiet and barely spoke. The other partner has a sarcastic nature and did not exhibit enthusiasm or optimism. He spent most his presentation "educating" the prospective buyers with an emphasis on all of the risks inherent to his business. He continually pointed out mistakes that should be avoided. He said that his goal was to be completely transparent but the end result of this approach is that the interested buyers became more cautious.

After the meetings, the best LOI that was received carried a $12 million valuation, $500,000 below the low-end of the bid range. Nothing else changed between the bid and receipt of the LOI other than the management meeting. By emphasizing only the risks associated with running this business, the meetings cost the owners $2 million.

Better preparation could have achieved a higher valuation. An honest discussion of risk can take place alongside an honest discussion of growth potential. With a rehearsal and feedback in a training session, sellers can learn how to project a story that emphasizes growth.

"The buyer knows what they are doing, they are educated on risk," Sekhon said. "If they want to know about the risks, they will do their due diligence and ask directly."

Selecting the Best Presenter

Many sellers have a difficult decision to make in deciding who is the best representative for the company. The answer is not always obvious. One of the roles Woodbridge's closers can play for sellers is to help sellers work through those decisions.

"We can be bankers, but we can also be management consultants and work with you on strategy," said Wallace. It is not uncommon for the sellers and the deal closer to have a conversation about the roles that members of the management team can play. Frequently, owners need help in making that decision.

Wallace has had 3-way conversations with a seller and one of the key managers to prepare for the meetings and used that conversation to evaluate the effectiveness of the manager as a presenter.

"We can discuss the situation and provide an opinion on whether the person has the skill set needed for the meetings," he said. "And if they don't, we can go to the next option."

Owners can be the best presenter but they often need coaching.

Derek Avdul, Woodbridge Director, recently told a group of sellers at a training session about a series of management meetings where two partners learned to improve their presentation skills, but they did it in front of potential buyers. At the first management meeting, the partners went off track telling stories that were tangential to the goal of selling the business. Avdul said it was obvious that the buyer's enthusiasm waned during the meeting and they did not submit an LOI. Fortunately for these partners, they had received several bids and held multiple management meetings. They took advantage of this opportunity to receive coaching and changed their approach. In subsequent management meetings, they stayed on track and presented a story of growth. Their performance improved with each meeting and so did the bids.

If these partners had attended the Woodbridge Management Training Workshop, they could have worked through these issues in a private session and made the best use of each management meeting instead of learning in front of a buyer.

Addressing the Human Factor

The buyer is looking for a strong ROI, but they know that they'll achieve it only if the team is solid. It has been said that 60% or more of the reason for the management meeting is to evaluate the people. The buyers need to be convinced that a team will continue to add value post-sale.

And there's the human factor. The buyers are going to be involved with the team that remains for several years. They don't want to be in business with people they don't like. And, perhaps most important, they are looking for people who are receptive to their opinions.

This can be a rude awakening for some business owners who have become accustomed to operating as the king of the castle. It is important to show a sense of humility with the buyers, especially if you are going to continue in the business during a transition or on a long-term basis. If you project a sense of arrogance, they will look at you as non-coachable.

Wallace advises sellers that it's OK to admit the business has limitations.

"Sometimes, being open about a weakness can be a difficult thing," said Wallace. "But these guys and gals are smart enough that they can figure it out anyway."

Some of the people you'll meet have bought hundreds of companies. They are not expecting the sellers to be perfect. And they're going to know from this meeting if you are not self-aware or that you are not aware of your limitations and your company's limitations.

Admitting that weaknesses exist in your business can be a way of demonstrating that you're going to be a good partner. In fact, recognizing limitations can be advantageous. Buyers are looking for an opportunity to add value. If you can admit that the company has been weak in marketing, for example, they'll see this as a void that can be filled with additional resources. Of course, if your company is great at marketing, it should be emphasized.

"Especially if you are going to stay on, buyers want to see a willingness to admit that you're not perfect and to hear you say, 'here's how you can help us grow.' Buyers always look for ways to add value."

- Bryan Wallace
Woodbridge Director

However, if the management team is strong enough it will be OK. Buyers want to buy turnkey businesses if the future story is strong.

Reinforcing the Ongoing Role of Your Management Team

Whether you are planning to leave the business immediately after the sale or after a period of transition, the buyers will need assurances that the remaining management team is competent and will be committed to continuing on in the business.

Many owners begin the process of selling their mid-sized business without informing their senior managers, preferring to hold off the discussion until the last possible moment. Each business is different, and the issues surrounding disclosure to the management staff need to be considered carefully. It is another area where Woodbridge's closers are able to provide guidance.

During Management Training Workshops, sellers are able to have frank discussions on the topic. A central question is whether the management meetings will be more effective if managers are brought into the discussion.

Meetings are more effective when key managers are brought in to present and reinforce the future story, and treating key managers with respect helps them stay motivated to carry on post-closing. Many sellers have found that their fears of telling their top people about the sale turn out to be unfounded. When proper assurances are given, managers can approach the sale as an opportunity to advance their career.

Woodbridge closers can provide you with background on some of the strategies available for retaining your best people through the sales process such as the following:

- **Golden-handcuff insurance policies**. These are a form of life insurance with an investment component. The beneficiary is the employee's family and the dividends are paid to the employee after a set period, such as five or 10 years. They can be an inexpensive vehicle to provide key staff members with an incentive to remain with the company before and after the sale.

- **Stay bonus**. These are straightforward bonus plans that can help retain employees before and after a sale. They work best when they are structured with specific goals over a period of time. They should never be tied to a sale, such as a payout on conclusion of a sale, as that would be a bright red flag for a buyer.

- **The post-sale opportunity.** One of the best strategies for motivating your key people costs nothing: Emphasize that the sale of your company is an opportunity for them. Key employees will be very important to the buyer, and with the additional resources flowing into the enterprise, they should find a bright career path.

"If it's a private equity platform, they want the employees, they're buying it to grow the company. They need the employees and they'll be adding employees," explains Buchholtz. "If it's a strategic buyer, the employees will be part of a bigger organization with more opportunity for them."

One of the opportunities that the senior management team and an owner who stays on after the sale may receive is an offer of equity in the new venture.

"Virtually every private equity deal sets aside equity for management," said Buchholtz. "Up to 5% or 15% of the equity gains go to the management teams. They're actually going to give management a much bigger opportunity than they had."

In many cases, the discussions with key staff about the sale can wait until a decision is made on who will attend the management meetings with buyers.

If your managers are not needed for these discussions, you will still want them to have some knowledge so they are prepared and enthusiastic about working for new owners. Remember that it is important your presentations educate the buyer on the reliable and talented team that is capable of running the business after the sale.

So you need to be prepared in advance. In a recent transaction closed by Woodbridge, the failure to have all key staff committed to a sale almost derailed a deal.

The company is a supplier to the government with a number of long-term contracts. The business has several highly compensated salespeople who have been with the company for many years whom the owners considered to be virtually family. The salespeople were an important part of telling the company's story and were needed in the management meetings.

The buyer was keen on keeping these salespeople and wanted them to sign employment agreements. As the transaction came to fruition and employment contracts were drafted, one of the salespeople demanded a 60% increase in her commission rate. She refused to sign a contract without her pound of flesh and the deal was being held hostage. Ultimately, the deal closed with the salesperson employed but without a contract. The future of these salespeople could have been dealt with upfront, prior to the moment of truth, with a stay bonus and an assignable contract.

Chapter 7: Your KPIs: The Comparison to Your Competitors

By now, we hope you have come to appreciate the connection between telling a growth story and your goal of achieving maximum value for your business. To tell that growth story convincingly, buyers need to project optimism and keep their focus on growth during the management meetings. As Woodbridge's team has seen over and over, sellers lose interest when they don't see enthusiasm radiating from the seller and their team.

But there is more to the sales process than just presenting the story. The story needs to be backed up with hard data if it is going to carry a business from bid to LOI and through the due diligence process. Even when a buyer is filled with enthusiasm, before they are ready to close the sale they will take a very careful look at the numbers they are given.

For many owners of medium-sized businesses, this may be the first time their numbers have been held up to close scrutiny. So, it is worth taking the time to prepare a bulletproof story that will help pave the way for a smooth closing.

"It's very easy to build a financial model, apply a growth rate on an annual basis, expand your margins a bit and before you know it, you have a projection," Bryan Wallace said. "But savvy buyers are going to toss all that out the window and build a metrics-based model that builds to revenue."

In this chapter, we're going to take a look at how the Woodbridge team is providing its clients with guidance during this process.

The Snowball Effect

In telling a growth story, it's important to consider the impact of momentum. All business people share an appreciation for the value of having momentum in a growing market. Like the growth in the size of a snowball rolling downhill, sales momentum is one of the most important ingredients in building a business. And buyers are always looking for evidence that a business has momentum. They want to believe that there is a snowball effect taking place in the business, with the potential to accelerate revenue growth. The buyer wants to believe that in the years to come, momentum will build and the business will not just grow, but scale up to achieve outsized growth.

Many sellers need to adjust their perspective in order to describe their business this way. There is a tendency among entrepreneurs toward conservative planning. They are managing the business for an immediate return and that requires a careful eye on expenses. The annual profit is often used to pay the owners a bonus, rather than serve as capital for expansion. The goal is a solid foundation that will provide steady income.

A growth story is different. Profits are re-directed back into the business in order to take market share from competitors or to bring new products to market.

Buyers are looking for a significant return on their investment, not a modest return. If they were interested in playing it safe to achieve a small profit, they could buy Treasury bills. To achieve maximum value for your own contribution, you need to help the buyer see the full potential. But you will need to use more than words. You'll need to provide metrics.

Demonstrating Growth Through KPIs

It is rare that the owners of a medium-size business are tracking a broad range of KPIs (Key Performance Indicators) on a consistent basis. Generally, the owners are focused on only a few numbers which they track religiously. Typically, they closely watch sales of the key products and controllable expenses. In preparing to tell the future story, the owners of medium-sized businesses are likely to take those basic financial metrics and build forecasts on historical trends.

A buyer is interested in financial projections, but they will also insist on knowing the metrics for all of the activities that underlie the business operations. If you sell widgets, they'll want to know more than just how many were sold this year vs. last year. They'll want to know whether the sales of blue widgets are growing compared with the red widgets. What was the breakdown of widget sales by region? Did you track revenue by sales channel? Sales through offline marketing vs. online marketing? What are the trends in the price paid for each ingredient in the widget recipe?

"In all of the deals I've had, the key piece of information every buyer asks for is to see the management dashboard," said Rez Mahboubi. "Every single one."

As you might imagine, it can be embarrassing for a seller who has to admit that they don't have one. No seller wants to be caught off guard when standing in front of a group that has expressed its willingness to buy their company. But many sellers have gone through that unfortunate experience.

That's why Woodbridge's Management Meeting Workshops include a discussion of how to present KPIs to a buyer. Attendees learn about the qualities that define a good KPI dashboard and gain insight into how buyers will view them. Remember, Woodbridge's deal closers are ready to act as a consultant and strategist to help their clients present their story.

Once a KPI dashboard is created, it can also help the business stay on track and in line with the buyer's expectations. The KPIs will keep the organization focused on the most important priorities. And that can keep the performance strong during an especially sensitive time. Buyers will be interested in knowing how the business is doing right until the day of closing.

When a seller is able to create a credible story for improving KPIs, it provides the Woodbridge team with extra ammunition to help drive up the valuation of your company.

At a recent workshop, attendees learned how a service company worked with the Woodbridge team to develop a strong KPI dashboard that included the data points below. Before they started working with Woodbridge, they were tracking only the number of customers and the average revenue per customer. After a brainstorming session, they developed a KPI dashboard that tracked these metrics:

- Number of new customers per month
- Number of cancelled customers per month
- Percentage of customer churn by week and month
- Average customer contract length (days active)
- Customer service: number of service calls
- Customer service: caller abandonment rate.

Using the metrics available through this newly created dashboard, the presentation that was made available to buyers included a "customer waterfall analysis" that could accurately forecast future revenue and EBITDA.

Sellers are often proud of their customer service record. They are ready to go in front of a buyer and claim that they have the best customer service in their market. But unless there are metrics that can be seen by a buyer, this claim will be subjected to intense questioning. Buyers will want to know how you reach this conclusion. Which metrics demonstrate good customer service?

"A savvy buyer will always ask a seller to prove what you're saying is true, and if you don't have the data, you're forcing them to take you at your word and that's a tricky position to be in," said Bryan Wallace.

Another book we suggest reading is *Measure What Matters: OKRs: The Simple Idea that Drives 10x Growth* by John Doerr. Every company should operate with OKRs (Objectives and Key Results) as a guiding principle.

Filling the Gaps In Your Story

If you put yourself in the position of a buyer, you would also assign no value to a purported growth factor where there is no hard evidence of how this potential will be converted into real revenue.

The importance of having metrics available to support your growth story is especially important when the buyers are private equity funds. And since private equity buyers are often willing to pay more for a business than a strategic buyer, it is worth the extra time and effort to gather the best data possible.

Private equity funds employ teams of number crunchers who will go through all of the financial statements and forecasts that a seller provides. The teams may spend days doing nothing but analyzing your numbers. Private equity buyers will come to the management meetings with a series of questions based on those analytics.

"We have to make sure that our data is not only accurate but it confirms the story," Wallace said.

One example of how this situation can play out in a management meeting is when a seller tells potential buyers that the company is poised to grow because it has excess capacity.

A buyer could consider excess capacity an asset that should have future value. But buyers will ask to hear the strategy that will take this asset and generate more revenue. If the seller is not prepared with a strong case, the buyer will be quick to assign zero value to extra capacity.

The Woodbridge team often needs to work through this type of issue with sellers. The first step is to identify the gaps in the story. Then, working with real metrics, a seller is often able to provide a more solid foundation to back up their growth story.

With solid metrics and a strategy for growth in hand, Woodbridge clients are in a much better position to achieve their own goals of selling their business at maximum value and having no regrets.

> "You come in with a certain amount of preconceived notions and you think you're prepared to meet with a buyer, but you're really not. The experience opened our eyes to a whole different kind of thinking and to things that we need to do to be prepared."
>
> *- Healthcare company owner who recently attended a Woodbridge Management Meeting Workshop with his partner*

Chapter 8: Risk Mitigation: Getting to the Finish Line

Many medium-sized businesses are able to attract bids from interested buyers, but somewhere along the line the buyers lose interest and the deal doesn't close. In this chapter, we'll talk about some of the reasons why this can happen and how Woodbridge helps clients avoid this fate.

Remember the 150-day timeline we discussed in Chapter 2? When a seller is willing to commit to meeting the milestones on the timeline, the odds are greatly improved for moving smoothly from marketing through bids to LOI and on to closing. Time is the enemy and delay is a relentless killer of deals.

The need to stay on schedule becomes especially critical after buyers have demonstrated their interest in making the acquisition. In Chapters 1 through 6, we talked about the steps that can showcase your company in the best light so it receives the best valuation.

But to make it to the finish line, we need to manage the buyer's sense of risk. Once a buyer has determined that a potential acquisition is attractive and they have established a valuation, they will always turn to questions around risk. Is the risk reasonable or is it excessive?

"Time allows people to second guess. It allows people to be influenced by outside forces. Time allows people to take what was once a logical course of action and convince themselves it was illogical. And in nearly all cases, the longer it takes to close a deal, the more that gets negotiated away or dies."

- Robert Koenig, CEO Woodbridge International

Surprises Cause Uncertainty

When buyers are able to see a clear view of the company and can review data to back up all projections, they have a lower sense of risk in buying a company. Familiarity fosters a sense of comfort.

A common problem for many sellers is a tendency to avoid discussing the risks that exist in their business in the hope that they will go unnoticed.

"The people we're going to be talking to don't miss things," Bryan Wallace advises Woodbridge clients. "It is in our interest to figure out the potential risks upfront so that they impact value as little as possible."

One of the attributes that buyers are looking for is the ability to face issues head on and resolve them as quickly as possible. No deal happens without trust. A great book on trust is *Trust Factor: The Science of Creating High-Performance Companies* by Paul Zak. Trust is at the core of every deal.

As an example of how this can be approached, consider the case of a Woodbridge client who had a business with strong sales, generating an attractive positive cash flow. It appeared to be a solid business, but in preparing the management presentations, it became clear that there was an underlying problem: Customer churn was very high. If the problem was not resolved, eventually the company would run out of new business and the cash flow would turn negative.

Rather than attempt to hide this challenge when meeting buyers, the seller collaborated with his Woodbridge closer and came to management meetings ready to discuss possible solutions to the problem. The presentation included slides with data on customer retention and a slide titled "Mitigating Churn." The result is that the topic lead to lively discussion with the potential buyers about the best way to fix the problem.

Buyers are willing to see a problem as an opportunity to add value. In this case, they could see that as customer retention improves, EBITDA rises over the current projections. The buyer who ultimately signed the LOI is moving ahead with confidence that they can improve customer renewals.

"If you know there is something that you're not doing perfectly, let's discuss it early," Wallace advises clients, "so that we can position it properly."

If the seller had attempted to hide the customer churn problem, it is almost certain that the buyers would have identified it as an issue during their due diligence. At that point, trust would have eroded and the buyers would have been less receptive to arguments that the problem can be fixed.

Woodbridge can't make risk go away, but it can help manage the risk. And it is also important to consider the value of maintaining credibility. Buyers will be far more comfortable entering into an agreement with an owner who is being upfront and not trying to hide any flaws. No deal happens without trust between the buyer and seller.

Mitigating Risk Factors

All businesses have weaknesses and underlying risks. And experienced investors understand that risk and reward go hand in hand. All you need to do is observe the equity markets gyrate from day to day. The biggest financial rewards come with risk.

Buyers of medium-sized companies understand that they will be taking on risk but are determined to take on as little risk as necessary.

In preparing management presentations, the Woodbridge team works with clients to help identify the weaknesses that need to be brought into the discussion. The following are common areas that buyers will want to explore:

- **Competition.** Be prepared to have frank discussions about your competitors. Don't be shy about admitting what they are doing better than you. Winning the battle against competitors is another potential area for the buyer to grow market share and improve future ROI.

- **Employee retention.** Strategic buyers may be considering consolidation with their own operations, but financial investors want to be assured that the current team is productive and prepared to stay on after the sale. Even if a strategic buyer is planning consolidation, they don't want to start out with human resource challenges. Buyers will expect to have a frank conversation about senior management and may require one-on-one meetings before closing the deal.

- **Customer satisfaction.** Buyers often perform their own research to determine if customers will be loyal. Woodbridge advises clients to perform customer satisfaction surveys and to be prepared to share the results with buyers. Woodbridge stands ready to provide this service on behalf of the seller.

- **Family members.** Many small businesses employ relatives of the owners. Proper disclosure of these relationships should be made early in the process. The owners should be prepared to discuss how their roles will be filled post-sale.

The biggest risk that a buyer faces is uncertainty. Any known risk factor or weakness can be assessed and assigned a value. Throughout the due diligence phase, the buyer is always on the lookout for new risks. When you disclose as much as you can early on, you reduce their sense of risk.

Consider the risk that was involved in this recent Woodbridge transaction:

The members of a third-generation manufacturing business decided to sell after the death of one of the shareholders. The deceased shareholder's assets were in probate and the executor of the estate had to agree to the sale and distribution of the assets.

As the transaction proceeded towards closing, the primary beneficiary of the estate, who was a shareholder and CFO of the company, passed away, throwing the entire transaction into question. Without the CFO to provide required diligence material, the transaction ground to a halt. With a single person as the keeper of all information, this deal had significant risk.

This was a predictable and avoidable problem that could have been dealt with prior to going to market. The transaction closed after much hand-wringing and legal activity, but steps could have been taken at the beginning of the process to be better prepared for the scrutiny of the due diligence process.

Another family business entered the sales process without resolving issues among shareholders, jeopardizing the sale. This family of two brothers, a sister and their mother were involved in a clothing manufacturing business that the mother started decades before. The business had prospered and all family members had done quite well, but the domestic garment business is not what it once was and the business had slipped. Relationships among the family members had deteriorated, further handicapping the business.

This situation continued for years with some family members wanting to sell the company and others not wanting to let it go. Finally, Woodbridge was hired and brought the business to market. A perfect strategic buyer emerged with an all-cash offer. One obstinate family member decided that he would never sign the deal; he felt the family never gave him enough credit for his contributions. However, after much cajoling, the deal was signed and closed.

The best approach for a seller to take toward risk mitigation is to have a frank discussion with their Woodbridge team about any weaknesses early in the process.

Don't let weaknesses fester undisclosed until they are uncovered during the due diligence process. The sooner they are brought out into the open, the easier it will be to come up with the best approach toward reducing the risk factors and improving the likelihood of closing the deal at top valuation.

It is important that you have clarity on your culture:

- What makes your company unique?
- Is your company goal oriented?
- Is it like a family?
- Do you care about our colleagues?
- Do you know what your "why" is...why your company exists?
- Do you have a vision that everyone is embracing?

If you know what your core values are, they need to be protected and illuminated, discussed and promoted. At the same time, you need to stimulate progress.

Buyers want to know what makes a company what it is. What's the one thing your company is best in the world at? What is the most important takeaway?

We recommend several books that discuss these issues, including *Good to Great* by Jim Collins and *The One Thing* by Gary Keller and Jay Papasan.

Chapter 9: Meeting Projections Through Closing: Be Diligent About Due Diligence

Selling a business is a lot of extra work for the owner of a mid-sized business. Ninety days into the process, with an LOI in hand, many owners are both tired and exhilarated. But this is not the time to take a break.

Between the LOI signing and closing, the buyer is performing due diligence, reviewing all of the documents they've received very carefully. It is common for the buyer's team to ask questions at all hours of the day, weekends included.

It is of utmost importance that the seller does not take their eye off the business at this point. It is extremely important that there are no negative surprises.

The first 90 days of the 150-day timeline are focused on telling a story of growth based on your historical performance. Woodbridge collaborates with the sellers to build financial projections based on the trends they've identified and the performance achieved in the business.

As the sale moves closer to the finish line with a signed LOI in hand, those financial projections will receive even more scrutiny.

Hitting the Numbers

Buyers will build their long-term financial projections using the numbers they've been given. It may be done for their own internal planning or they may need to provide it to banks that are financing the deal. When the buyer is a private equity fund, the type of financial model they use will be based on the basic financial model the seller helped build. However, they will combine that with intricate formulas and assumptions that may be completely foreign territory to the seller.

"If you were to look at the models built by a private equity fund, you would be amazed at the level of detail they can build into the analysis," said Wallace.

Once the LOI is signed, the buyer will be asking for regular updates on the seller's performance, which they'll plug into their models.

"They are going to look long term," said Wallace, "and if there is a disconnect, it will affect valuation. You have to hit the numbers that are in the book. Buyers are bidding off those numbers, expecting them to be hit. We are, in effect, making a promise that this is the financial performance of the business. And as soon as we fall short of our promise, they will come back and say, 'That $15 million price? It's now $13.5 million. And here's why I'm adjusting the value.' It is important that your projections are aggressive but also achievable."

The projections made early in the process should be aggressive but achievable. If they're too low, you'll be losing out on the best valuation. But if they can't be achieved, the seller is setting the stage for a problem.

In one instance, a Woodbridge client projected a $14 million EBITDA for the current fiscal year ending December. As we got towards the closing date, it was not only apparent that the annual EBITDA would be more like $12.7 million, but the most recent quarter had only $2 million of EBITDA.

The buyer tried to make the case that they should not reduce the price by only 9.3% (which would reflect a change of $1.3 million/$14 million) but by a much larger amount since $2 million over four quarters equals a run-rate of $8 million of EBITDA, not $12.7 million annually. Rather than even have a discussion about price, it would have been far easier if the client had met its $14 million projection to begin with.

The deal did close, with a small adjustment, not the large one the buyer argued for. But if there had been no miss on EBITDA, we would have been able to avoid a discussion about renegotiating price altogether.

Once again, regular communication with your Woodbridge closer is essential. The sooner any missed targets are identified, the easier it will be to take corrective action. If adjustments need to be made to the model, the Woodbridge team will get to work.

At the LOI signing, the buyer will be paying particular attention to the most recent month's financial performance. From this point through the closing, every month's performance will matter. If there are explanations that reduce the significance of a decline, that's information that should be conveyed and it may help to reduce the buyer's concerns.

The seller can't take their foot off the gas now. The signing of the LOI is the start of the home stretch and as any race fan knows, this is the time when races are won or lost.

The Closing Mindset

The job is not finished until the paperwork is done. And there is a lot of paperwork involved in closing the sale of a business. As an entrepreneur, you may be comfortable operating on your gut, but the lawyers and financial analysts at private equity firms and banks are not. They operate by reviewing documents. Lots of documents.

Woodbridge advises clients to take on a closing mindset. Be ready to answer questions and to supply more documents than you think necessary. In addition, it's essential that the seller is available to answer questions throughout the period. Vacations can wait until after closing.

You should be prepared to approach the closing with a "do or die" mindset. Be prepared to do whatever it takes to close the deal. That does not mean you need to make concessions. Far from it. Your Woodbridge closer is prepared to work with you as a partner to ensure that you get the best deal. And the best way to do that is to have a firm approach toward closing the deal on your terms. If you are prepared to approach the closing date as a firm deadline, the buyer will sense your determination and reciprocate.

Think of the closing date as a set-in-stone wedding date. Work with us to make sure all lawyers and all advisors think that way. We had one client who asked for a $3 million penalty: If the buyer didn't close on that date, it would cost them $3 million more. Don't you think the deal closed on that date?

One responsibility for the seller is to ride hard on your team and make sure that they are not creating obstacles. Don't let your own lawyers slow down the process. A good practice is to schedule weekly meetings with everyone on your team who is involved with the closing. Pay attention to all of the items on the timeline and see to it that they are being addressed quickly.

Pay attention to the requests for documents that need to be made available in the data room, which is a secure website accessible only to the parties involved in the deal. The seller's team will be responsible for supplying contracts, leases, accounting statements and other documents so they can be seen by the buyer's team. The seller needs to treat these document requests seriously. If the data room is not complete, it will slow the process and leave the seller vulnerable.

We have a weekly "all-hands call" with everyone involved in a deal. Everyone is asked to report on progress, and to provide an accounting of items that need to be completed.

That does not mean you will need to answer questions from the buyers endlessly. Some buyers go overboard with questions. In many deals, Woodbridge's closers need to send the buyer a clear message that the time for questions is over.

Adequate preparation is the key to achieving the best outcome. Here is an example:

The owner of a chemical distributor in the Northeast hired Woodbridge to sell his business. He was a talented salesman who had built a substantial business, and although relatively young, it was time for him to cash out.

Prior to hiring Woodbridge, he had hired a pair of consultants who had helped him prepare his company for sale. Documentation, financial information, legal were all clean as a whistle. The reception to his business in the marketplace was phenomenal. Numerous financial and strategic buyers were ready to beat down the door to own this business. A highly competitive auction ensued.

The owner walked away with almost twice the amount of money he expected. He had built his company over a number of years, prepared it well, and the market gave him real kudos. The deal closed 150 days from the day Woodbridge was hired. This owner's sense of success and victory were immeasurable. He did what he had set out to do, finish big, and he had no regrets.

Once again, the 150-day timeline helps to maintain momentum. Woodbridge establishes the closing date in the beginning of the process for good reasons. A strict schedule provides all parties with adequate time to do their jobs but it prevents unnecessary delay from endangering the sale.

In his book *Good to Great: Why Some Companies Make the Leap...and Others Don't,* Jim Collins talks about starting with the end in mind and then working backwards. A goal without a deadline is just a dream.

Due diligence is a necessary process and it requires a certain amount of time. But Woodbridge's team will not allow it to be used as an excuse to delay the closing. Sellers who can work cooperatively to that purpose give their deal every chance for success.

Chapter 10: Ready to Sell: Going to Market with an Understanding of the Buyer's Perspective

By now, you should have a good idea of how buyers will be looking at your business. Even more important, you know how you can be prepared to meet their expectations. Every deal is different, but the process of selling a medium-sized business doesn't change all that much from one deal to the next.

The following are some of the more important lessons that we've covered and that bear emphasizing:

- **Commit to the 150-day Timeline.** Woodbridge created the timeline to build a competitive auction around your business. Each step along the way is helping to set the stage for closing at a maximum valuation. But delay undermines the process by adding uncertainty. To achieve the best outcome for yourself, the company, your family and all concerned, you need to be committed to following the process. And you need to make sure that the people on your team deliver on their obligations. Time kills deals.

- **Create Projections That Are Aggressive and Achievable**. During the first 40 days, you'll need to work with the Woodbridge underwriting team to create financial projections that will be used by buyers to establish the valuation. Be thoughtful in preparing projections you can commit to throughout the process.

  Develop projections that do not sell you short, yet won't put you in the position of having to explain why you missed your numbers.

- **Create a Growth Story.** Woodbridge's professional writers will create a book that describes your company in positive terms, but the owners need to identify the growth factors. Be ready to discuss new initiatives that would be successful if additional resources become available. The buyer is looking at your business with an eye toward substantial growth. Help them imagine the possibilities. Be ready to show data that can be extrapolated for growth.

- **Know Why Your Company Exists – Now and in the Future.** Be prepared to present the vision for your company. Recognize that buyers are looking for a company that was built to last. Does your company solve problems that will need to be solved for the long term? The following page shows the "Whys" as defined by some leading companies:

The "Why" of major companies

Available at
amazon

Amazon

To be **earth's most customer-centric** company; to build a place where people can come to find and discover anything they might want to buy online.

Coca-Cola

To Refresh the world in mind, body & spirit

Disney

To make people happy.

Walt Disney

Google

To provide access to the world's information in one click.

Uber

To make transportation as reliable as running water everywhere for everyone.

9

- **Identify Key People Who Should Be in The Room to Present.** Be ready to share the stage with your top managers. You need to sell your management team as committed partners in the enterprise who are ready to continue building profits in the years after the sale. Identify what it takes to be part of your team. Be prepared to talk about the type of person who works at your company and why they are attracted to it.

- **Share Your Enthusiasm for the Business.** Be prepared to share the passion that led you to start the business and persevere over the years. The buyers want to see enthusiasm from the owners and a sense of optimism about future potential. Your enthusiasm should shine through in the management meetings – along with your presentation of the facts and KPIs that demonstrate how success was achieved.

How we know the business is in control

KPI's key performance indicators

Criteria	1	2	3	4	5	6
Steps 1-7						
Escalating after 3 calls						
Introductions 1/week						
Testimonials 1/month						

- **Perform a Gap Analysis to Identify Risks.** Buyers understand they are taking on risk when they acquire a business but they work hard to minimize the risk. Be prepared to discuss the weaknesses that exist in your business today and in the future. What are the gaps between where you are and where you want to be? Don't expect to skate through the due diligence phase without an examination that reveals every challenge the business faces. Demonstrate leadership by being prepared to explain the challenges and how they can be overcome.

- **Keep Your Foot on the Gas.** While you're taking part in discussions about the sale, it's important that the business maintain momentum. This is not the time to take your eye off the main business drivers. Be sure the team is motivated to hit the revenue and expense numbers in your projections.

- **Be Ready to Supply the Data Room with all Requested Documents.** The buyer's attorneys and analysts will require extensive documentation and copies of all legally binding agreements. Don't allow the paperwork to slow down the deal. Take advantage of attorneys who work with Woodbridge and who will be aligned with you and can protect you with fixed fees.

- **Schedule Weekly Calls.** Stay on top of your lawyers, accountants and everyone else involved in the sale to make sure that you're meeting all of your obligations. Don't allow your team to be the cause for delays.

- **Adopt a Closing Mindset.** Approach the closing with a "do or die" attitude. Be prepared to do whatever it takes to make the deal that you want. Your Woodbridge team will be prepared to stand shoulder-to-shoulder and make that happen. Treat the scheduled closing date on your 150-day timeline as if it were set in stone. Do not allow your team to slow down during the due diligence process. Don't schedule vacations between the management meetings and closing. Stay focused on the details. Be prepared to answer questions within 24 hours. Don't allow external forces to prevent you from achieving the best deal possible.

- **Fixed-Fee Agreements with Lawyers.** One of the most important people you will need to help close your deal is an M&A attorney. Woodbridge has negotiated fixed-fee agreements only for our clients with four major M&A law firms. These firms have closed many deals on behalf of Woodbridge clients, and they are incentivized to close the deals on the closing date once an LOI is signed. They have zero incentive to create obstacles and additional billable hours. We strongly recommend you interview them.

Achieving a Positive Transformation in Your Life

We hope this book has been helpful to you as you prepare to bring your business to market.

We believe that sharing what our team has learned over the years can help all business owners understand the dynamics of selling their business. And we will continue to provide educational resources that help business owners achieve their goals.

Woodbridge is committed to helping our clients achieve a positive transformation in their lives.

After 25 years of selling companies of all types, we've developed a comprehensive M&A program that helps owners avoid the common pitfalls experienced by many sellers who end up regretting their situation after a sale.

Our process is designed to educate sellers so they will have multiple bidders to choose from, and they will be able to close a deal with the best buyer. Our big, bold thinking and marketing on your behalf and our dedicated team of domain experts are working with the most innovative program in M&A today. We're using the most advanced techniques to market our clients and are providing a level of education that gives our clients a unique advantage. Our management training workshops go far beyond the level of attention that is being offered by any other firm in the world of M&A.

We want to see our clients sign a deal that provides them with a value that exceeds their expectations and places their company with a buyer who will treat their colleagues well. Your company should have a legacy that lives on after the sale. Work with us and you'll be proud of the legacy that your company represents while you enjoy a positive transformation in your own life.

The Woodbridge process is designed to bring your company to more buyers and position your future story in the best light. We want you to enjoy the best possible outcome and finish big with no regrets. And that only happens when you have choice.

We look forward to working with you and helping you achieve your goals.

Recommended Reading

Woodbridge is committed to sharing knowledge and creating a culture of lifelong learning. To that end, we recommend the following books as worthy of your time and attention:

“Good to Great: Why Some Companies Make the Leap...and Others Don't” by Jim Collins

“Built to Last: Successful Habits of Visionary Companies” by Jim Collins

“The E Myth: Why Most Businesses Don't Work and What to Do About It” by Michael E. Gerber

“Measure What Matters: How Google, Bono & the Gates Foundation Rock the World with OKRs” by John Doerr

“Explosive Growth: A Few Things I Learned While Growing To 100 Million Users - And Losing $78 Million” by Cliff Lerner

“Trust Factor: The Science of Creating High-Performance Companies” by Paul J. Zak

“The ONE Thing: The Surprisingly Simple Truth Behind Extraordinary Results” by Gary Keller

“Innovating: A Doer’s Manifesto” by Luis Perez-Breva

“Start With Why: How Great Leaders Inspire Everyone to Take Action” by Simon Sinek

Chapter 11: Four Case Studies of Clients who Finished Big with No Regrets

Case Study 1: Athletica Sports Systems acquired by Fulcrum Capital Partners

Seller. Canada-based Athletica Sport Systems is the world leader in the design, manufacture, sale and installation of branded aluminum dasher board systems for hockey arenas and indoor athletic facilities. Athletica has 16 patents and 16 trademarks, with registrations in the U.S., Canada and Russia. With more than 3,000 installations worldwide and brand legacy reaching back over 50 years, dasher boards and most other products are designed and manufactured at Athletica's 73,000-square-foot headquarters facility in Waterloo, which includes 60,000 square feet of production and warehouse space.

Robert Naegele Jr., as a serial entrepreneur, has a long history of transforming major global branded companies including Rollerblade Inc., Mission Hockey, the Minnesota Wild and now Athletica Sport Systems. The strong management team members assembled by Mr. Naegele were ready to remain after a sale and take the company to the next level of success.

Buyer. Private equity firm Fulcrum Capital presented the winning bid. They saw in Athletica a well-run company with professional management that was successful in turning the company around. They liked its dominant position in its marketplace and the fact that it had good organic and inorganic growth opportunities. Paul Eldridge, a Partner at Toronto-based Fulcrum Capital, said about the acquisition, "The company's reputation for superior customer service, safety and industry-leading solutions make Athletica an exciting investment for Fulcrum. We plan to build upon the solid foundation created by the team at Athletica."

The Team on the Athletica Sport Systems Deal

A Woodbridge team of 17 people worked on the Athletica deal. They were:

Auction Results

Total # of Buyer Contacts	# of Strategics	# of PEGs	# of Books Out	# of Days Launch to Close	# of Bids	# of LOIs	Buyers who attended Mgt. Meetings	Buyers Submitting LOIs
21,081	15,000	6,018	119	174	14	5	• PEG, Miami, FL • PEG with strategic, Minneapolis, MN • Strategic, Mill Valley, CA • PEG, Denver, CO • PEG, Tampa, FL • Strategic, Chicago, IL • Fulcrum Capital, Ontario, Canada	• Yes • Yes • No • Yes • No • Yes • Yes

Transaction Highlights

What were the reasons our client wanted to sell?	He was in his late 70s and this company was the last one he still owned and he was ready to retire.
Main reason our client chose the buyer they closed with	Fulcrum was funded (the others were unfunded), so Fulcrum's ability to close the deal was significantly higher than the other buyers.
Did our client stay on to run the business?	The owner did not, but the management team stayed.
Did our client roll equity?	The owner did not, but the management team did.
Did our client take back paper?	No. It was an all-cash deal.
Did we get our client more than they wanted for the business?	Yes - 20% more.
What were the obstacles that we needed to overcome?	An unfunded buyer seemed to be offering a higher price, but upon analyzing the offer more closely with our client, we advised him to accept the offer from the funded buyer, which in fact turned out to be higher – and offered our client certainty to close.

Marketing Associate Advocacy. As soon as interested buyers began contacting Woodbridge for a Confidentiality Agreement and the Athletica CIM, Justin Schaffer, Woodbridge Marketing Associate, went to work selling Athletica's key growth drivers to the book holders. Some of the value points he emphasized to buyers were:

Justin Schaffer
Marketing Associate

- Athletica's products are installed in 3,000 venues and all but one of the National Hockey League stadiums
- Company services equipment in 150 rinks
- Company was in the process of buying a company to grow their product offering by being able to provide steel dasher boards as well as expand their footprint
- Company's owner is a former NHL owner, brush shoulders with NHL owners.

Buyer Research Team Analysis. The research team brainstormed about which types of strategic buyers could fit with Athletica and developed this list of buyer categories shown on the following page.

Jesse **Abrahams**
Gassant **Richards**
Phozisa **Cabane**
Jason **Aubin**
Cape Town Researchers

Sporting and athletic goods, not elsewhere classified	Architectural metalwork	Stadium seating
Stadium construction	Athletic and recreation facilities construction	Ice surface maintenance: hockey, curling, etc.
Sporting and recreation goods	Refrigeration service and repair/ ice surfacing	Sports clubs, managers, and promoters
Architectural services: stadium, arena, ice rink, soccer, baseball	Concessionaire	Nonresidential building operators
Sporting and athletic goods manufacturing	Facilities management use with keywords "sports" "arenas"	Construction & engineering
Venue management	Sports	Arenas
Scoreboard	Digital signs	Hockey
Dasher board	Stadiums	Venues

Underwriting Overview. Kyle Richard, Woodbridge's Underwriting Director, conducted the underwriting on the Athletica deal. "Athletica had a sophisticated CEO/CFO team, overseen by an active Board of Directors. This translated into a business that was cleanly run, organized, modernized, and could produce timely and accurate data. Further, the company commissioned an annual financial statement audit (from a large, credible firm) which added a significant amount of trust and confidence in the financial results."

Kyle Richard
Director, Underwriting

Book Writer Insight. Steve Higgins wrote the Athletica book. He said, "I was impressed with the world-class clients Athletica serves. I was also impressed with the company's plans to expand its products and services into more community sports complexes and its diversification into new products such as enclosures including food kiosks, laboratory testing booths, pharmaceutical-grade divider walls, and more. Athletica management was easy to work with and quickly provided all the information needed to produce an effective memorandum book."

Steve Higgins
Book Writer

Closer Summary. Ash Savani, the Closer on the deal, observed that "Woodbridge ran a very effective and efficient auction which resulted in the sale of Athletica to Fulcrum Capital Partners, a Canadian private equity firm focused on the Canadian lower middle market. There were a few challenges from the LOI to close date, but we were successfully able to resolve the issues and close the transaction on the agreed upon date in the LOI."

Ash Savani
Closer

Why Our Client Finished Big and Had No Regrets. Our client received significantly more for his company than he expected – and was able to exit the business knowing he closed with the right buyer at the best price. That's how Woodbridge positively transformed our client Bob Naegele's life. We gave him a range of buyer options and he was extremely pleased with the outcome. You can watch his testimonial here: https://woodbridgegrp.com/testimonials.

Case Study 2: York Analytical Laboratories acquired by Terra Nova Partners

October 2018

York Analytical Laboratories, Inc.
Stratford, Connecticut

was acquired by

TerraNova Partners LP
Toronto, Ontario, Canada

The undersigned acted as advisor to York Analytical Laboratories, Inc.

Tel: 203.389.8400 • Web: woodbridgegrp.com
1764 Litchfield Turnpike, Suite 250, New Haven, CT 06525

Seller. York Analytical Laboratories is Greater New York's preeminent full-service environmental testing lab, servicing environmental consultants, developers, utilities, corporate entities and government agencies. York provides analysis of environmental samples including water, soil, air and drinking water for regulated contaminants. York is a NELAP-accredited laboratory and maintains comprehensive licenses in various states including Connecticut, New York, New Jersey and Pennsylvania. In addition to serving clients working on monitoring, commercial development and abatement projects, York is involved in large, long-term infrastructure and high-profile projects such as the La Guardia, JFK and Newark airport reconstructions, the Yankee Stadium development, and the Second Avenue Subway and Brooklyn Navy Yards projects. York is headquartered in Nyack, NY with labs in Stratford, CT and Queens, NY, and an additional facility in Prospect Park, NJ.

Michael (Mike) P. Beckerich, CEO and owner, has built York Analytical Laboratories into a highly respected and successful company. His son and President of York, Michael J. Beckerich, had been running the business for over 10 years and was eager to continue his leadership role in driving York to its next level of prosperity. Mike, the father, was less involved in day-to-day operations during the past two years and wanted to pursue other interests and retire.

Buyer. TerraNova Partners LP is a multi-disciplined and diversified investment fund focused primarily on private equity investments. The firm regarded York Analytical as an ideal platform acquisition. TerraNova believes that the success of a company is driven by the strength of the management team and the people within the organization. They really liked Michael and thought he could continue to grow the business. The firm was also attracted by York's Blue-Chip customer base, and they felt the niche of environmental testing was strong and ripe for multiple acquisitions. As part of their general investment thesis, TerraNova states, "We need to see a real advantage held by a company in its chosen industry and we must also be convinced that the management team, with our support and capital investment, will accelerate their business plan."

The Team on the York Analytical Labs Deal

A Woodbridge team of 17 people worked on the York deal. They were:

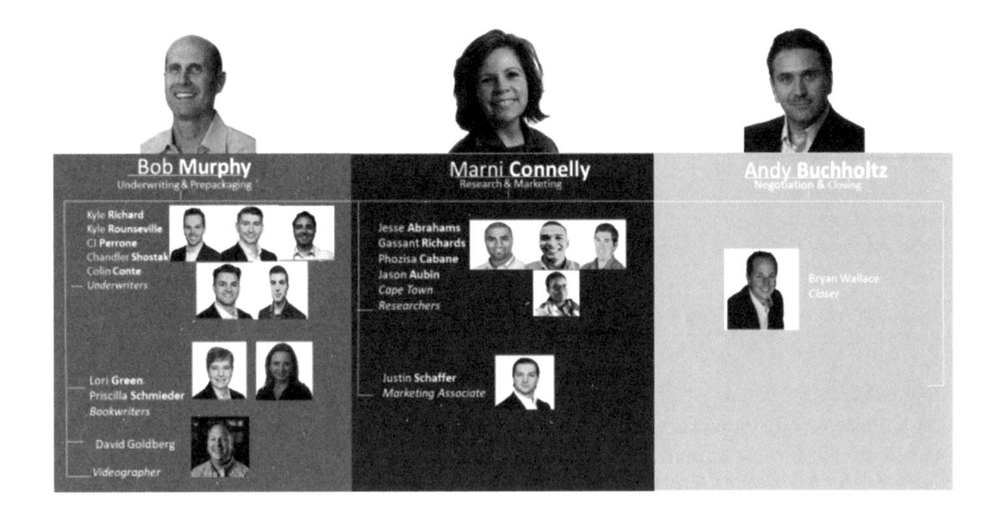

Auction Results

Total # of Buyer Contacts	# of Strategics	# of PEGs	# Books Out	# of Days Launch to Close	# of Bids	# of LOIs	Buyers who attended Mgt. Meetings	Buyers Submitting LOIs
21,697	15,679	6,018	207	169	49	7	• PEG, MA	• No
							• PEG, Tampa, FL	• No
							• Strategic, Jacksonville, FL	• No
							• PEG, Cleveland, OH	• No
							• TerraNova, Ontario, Canada	• Yes
							• Strategic, White Plains, NY	• Yes
							• PEG, Portola Valley, CA	• Yes
							• Strategic, Irvine, CA	• Yes
							• PEG, NYC	• Yes
							• PEG, Alexandria, VA	• Yes
							• PEG, Quincy, MA	

Transaction Highlights

What were the reasons our client wanted to sell?	The owner (father of CEO) wanted to move on to other opportunities and have his son stay to continue growing the business and carry on the legacy of success.
Main reason our client chose the buyer they closed with	The buyer's high bid and interest in keeping the owner's son in place, plus the buyer's willingness to sign a long-term lease on favorable economic terms combined to convince our client this was the right buyer.
Did our client stay on to run the business?	Client's son stayed on as President/CEO.
Did our client roll equity?	About 20%.
Did our client take back paper?	No.
Did we get our client more than they wanted for the business?	Yes – 50% more.
What were the obstacles that we needed to overcome?	Clearly demonstrating path to growth, persuading the buyer that the son had ability to run with business, and addressing the drawbacks related to the lack of back-office infrastructure and a controller.

Marketing Associate Advocacy. Justin Schaffer, Woodbridge Marketing Associate, sold TerraNova on the York Analytical opportunity by highllghting these unique features of the company to buyers:

Justin Schaffer
Marketing Associate

- NYC's #1 environmental service company with locations in CT and NJ
- Premium-level customer service
- 10-20 additional acquisition targets identified
- Company is growing rapidly
- Successful CEO will stay on
- Company won a major municipal project from a competitor by the CEO riding his bike to the site every week asking if he could help and bringing donuts. Eventually the site leader signed over the contract
- Company is a brand builder and puts York candy bars on all customers' desks!

Buyer Research Team Analysis. For York Analytical and all clients, we want to be as thorough as possible when researching prospective buyers. We included companies that fell in York's core industry of commercial research services, to highlight the prospect of a horizontal merger. We also went to peripheral industries such as environmental control equipment manufacturing, analytical instrument manufacturing and air, water and solid waste management services to cover all avenues for a possible vertical merger. The buyer categories are shown on the following page:

Jesse **Abrahams**
Gassant **Richards**
Phozisa **Cabane**
Jason **Aubin**
Cape Town Researchers

Highway and street construction, except elevated highways	Commercial physical research	Testing laboratories
Commercial nonphysical research	Noncommercial research organizations	Fluid meters and counting devices
Environmental controls	Process control instruments	Air, water, and solid waste management
Analytical instruments	Measuring and controlling devices	Commercial physical research
Pollution control equipment, water	Freight transportation arrangement	Testing laboratories
Refuse systems	Sanitary services	Heavy construction, except highway and street construction
Engineering services	Noncommercial research organizations	Commercial nonphysical research

Underwriting Overview. Underwriter Chandler Shostak was the point person on York Analytical. "York came to our kick-off meeting with a pre-packaged data room (on Day 7 of our process) eager to discuss its contents. The client's focus, preparedness and commitment allowed the underwriting team the opportunity to scrutinize potential deal issues, develop positioning (instead of chasing down documents), and act like a real buyer to prepare York for buyer scrutiny."

Chandler Shostak
Associate, Underwriting

Book Writer Insight. Priscilla Schmieder, one of Woodbridge's longtime book writers, wrote the York Analytical book. She said "York has an impressive overall business, marquis client base and proven track record working on large-scale construction sites. Setting up a lab in Queens was quite a feat due to regulatory requirements and higher costs, yet the company overcame these barriers and can now serve NY metro customers even better than before. The owners are fast-paced New Yorkers and we quickly received all the information we needed to write the book."

Priscilla Schmieder
Book Writer

Closer Summary. Bryan Wallace said, "We hit all three objectives for the client and achieved historical trading level of similar companies that normally trade at a multiple of 5.6 and this deal was 6.8 multiple. We encouraged the buyer to invest in the transaction and by the time the Quality of Earnings was done, the buyer had paid for transaction fees and expenses, allocated equity and were in advanced financing discussions. Most important: our client received more in value than he expected and couldn't have been more delighted."

Bryan Wallace
Closer

Why Our Client Finished Big and Had No Regrets. The seller's son remained with the company as President/CEO with a generous compensation package that included equity and stock options. The owner also received a long-term lease agreement on the main facility with favorable terms. After the deal closed, the owner was well prepared to transition into a new phase of his life with the resources and peace of mind he sought. The whole Woodbridge team was pleased to have positively transformed the life of this business owner.

Case Study 3: Fun Spot Manufacturing acquired by ABEO

October 2018

Fun Spot Manufacturing, LLC
Hartwell, Georgia

was acquired by

ABEO
Rioz, France

The undersigned acted as advisor to
Fun Spot Manufacturing, LLC

Tel: 203.389.8400 • Web: woodbridgegrp.com
1764 Litchfield Turnpike, Suite 250, New Haven, CT 06525

Seller. Hartwell, Georgia-based Fun Spot is a leading vertically integrated equipment designer and manufacturer for the fast-growing, active recreation parks market. With more than 750 Fun Spot-touched parks across the globe, the company serves a diverse customer base, a mix of franchisees and independent owners. From high-energy action to gravity-defying attractions, Fun Spot is at the forefront of innovation, redefining the trampoline park experience with a wide array of attractions and creative layouts that maximize ROI for the park operators. All products are manufactured, sold and distributed from two plants in Georgia, which house a total of 95,000 square feet.

Arch Adams is more comfortable in an entrepreneurial role than as the CEO of a sizable international company and felt it was in the best interest of the company and himself to sell the entity to a buyer capable of leading Fun Spot to the next level. Fun Spot's management team was excited about the transaction and fully committed to remain in place under new ownership.

Buyer. ABEO Group is a French corporation and world leader in sports and leisure equipment. The company markets its products in over 100 countries. ABEO Group CEO Olivier Estèves said, "This acquisition is fully in tune with the strategic ambitions we have set ourselves. It is aimed at strengthening ABEO's footprint on the North American continent and at developing our business in 'Sportainment', a future sector with major growth potential."

The Team on the Fun Spot Manufacturing Deal

A Woodbridge team of 17 people worked on the Fun Spot deal. They were:

Auction Results

Total # of Buyer Contacts	# of Strategics	# of PEGs	# of Days Launch to Close	# of Books Out	# of Bids	# of LOIs	Buyers who attended Mgt. Meetings	Buyers Submitting LOIs
13,000	6,199	6,801	153	257	26	5	• ABEO, Rioz, France	• Yes
							• PEG, Dallas, TX	• No
							• PEG, Boston, MA	• No
							• Strategic, Mumbai, India	• Yes
							• PEG, New York, NY	• Yes
							• Strategic, Newport Beach, CA	• No
							• PEG, Southport, CT	• Yes
							• PEG, Los Angeles, CA	• Yes

Transaction Highlights

What were the reasons our client wanted to sell?	He felt given Fun Spot's overall size and projected growth, the company would grow faster in the hands of a buyer with greater resources. He also wanted to focus on other ventures.
Main reason our client chose the buyer they closed with	He selected the offer with the best structure to suit his objectives. This offer was not the one with the highest price, but with the highest closing cash.
Did our client stay on to run the business?	No, but he did agree to be a part-time consultant for two years.
Did our client roll equity?	No.
Did our client take back paper?	No.
Did we get our client more than they wanted for the business?	Two main objectives achieved - all cash deal and no need to stay as CEO with the business post-transaction.
What were the obstacles that we needed to overcome?	The company was comprised of five legal entities in the U.S., Hong Kong and India, and its accounting was not GAAP compliant. There were also restrictive land-use covenants and outstanding legal disputes. All were overcome.

Marketing Associate Advocacy. Brie Campbell, Vice President, Client Marketing, was the Marketing Associate for the Fun Spot deal. She elicited a solid 10% yield of bids from the large number of book holders by staying in close contact with all of them and reminding them that:

Brie Campbell
VP, Client Marketing

- Fun Spot had a long family history, having been started by the seller's father
- Owner is extremely well-versed in the industry and knows his competition well
- Owner is a growth-driven entrepreneur who also founded Rush Parks, a major trampoline park.

Buyer Research Team Analysis. The research team brainstormed about which types of strategic buyers could fit with Fun Spot. For Fun Spot they included sporting goods manufacturers and retailers, recreational construction companies as well as all amusement facilities services to cover the possibility of a horizontal or vertical merger. The team's list of buyer categories are shown on the following page.

Jesse **Abrahams**
Gassant **Richards**
Phozisa **Cabane**
Jason **Aubin**
Cape Town Researchers

Sporting and athletic goods, not elsewhere classified	Playground construction and equipment installation	Carnival amusement park equipment
Sporting and recreation goods	Amusement arcade	Gyms and physical fitness facilities
Wire springs	Sporting and athletic goods manufacturing	Leisure products
Rubber floorcoverings/mats and wallcoverings	Sports and recreation instruction	Trampoline
Miscellaneous amusement and recreation services	Sporting goods manufacturing	Sport manufacturer
Sporting goods and bicycle shops	Plastic & rubber manufacturing	Amusement
Hobby, toy and game shops	Sporting and recreational camps	Playground
Court construction, indoor athletic	Playground equipment	Recreation

Underwriting Overview. "This client had several entities, complicated accounting and was not preparing monthly consolidated GAAP financial statements. We worked with the client over several months to properly prepare financial information that would stand up in buyer due diligence. The transaction was successfully completed as a result of being prepared for due diligence and the client having a great product."

Kyle Richard
Director, Underwriting

Book Writer Insight. Lisa Micali, a book writer with Woodbridge for over 10 years, said of her work on Fun Spot, "Fun Spot was a compelling offering not only because of its high-quality business and effective management team, but also due to brand and reputation among customers, suppliers and employees. They began aggressively reinvesting in plant expansion in order to capitalize on the burgeoning worldwide demand for their products and services."

Lisa Micali
Book Writer

Closer Summary. Rez Mahmoubi, the deal Closer, said, "There was a perfect fit between our client and this strategic buyer. Many other buyers just couldn't see what a robust future opportunity Fun Spot was, but ABEO did see the future - and liked what they saw." The Fun Spot acquisition is fully aligned with ABEO's strategic growth plans.

Rez Mahmoubi
Closer

Why Our Client Finished Big and Had No Regrets. The Woodbridge team is proud to have found the world's best buyer for Fun Spot, along with the price and structure that completely achieved our client's goals. We positively transformed our client's future by making it possible for him to finish big. He is delighted with the outcome and has zero regrets.

Case Study 4: Complete Packaging & Shipping Supplies acquired by Mitch Mankosa

Seller. Complete Packaging & Shipping Supplies is a New York-based large-scale distributor of hardware and tools, packaging supplies, electronics, office supplies and other products serving the U.S. government and commercial companies. Government sales account for 82% of sales, and the rest are to commercial customers. Since it was founded in 1990, the company has built enduring relationships with thousands of vendors and manufacturers, making Complete Packaging a true single-source for everything from office and janitorial supplies to technology products and building materials.

Founder Jeffrey Berkowitz wished to retire after building Complete Packaging into a thriving company with a growing, diverse client base and a strong foundation in supplying government agencies nationwide.

Buyer. Mitch Mankosa, a business executive with a background in packaging and a U.S. Army veteran, led a buyer group that is 50% veteran-owned, which will allow Complete Packaging to obtain veteran-owned/small business status in selling to its many government customers. Mitch is very excited to own the company and continue growing it to become the country's premier government supplier.

The Team on the Complete Packaging & Shipping Supplies Deal

A Woodbridge team of 17 people worked on the Complete Packaging deal. They were:

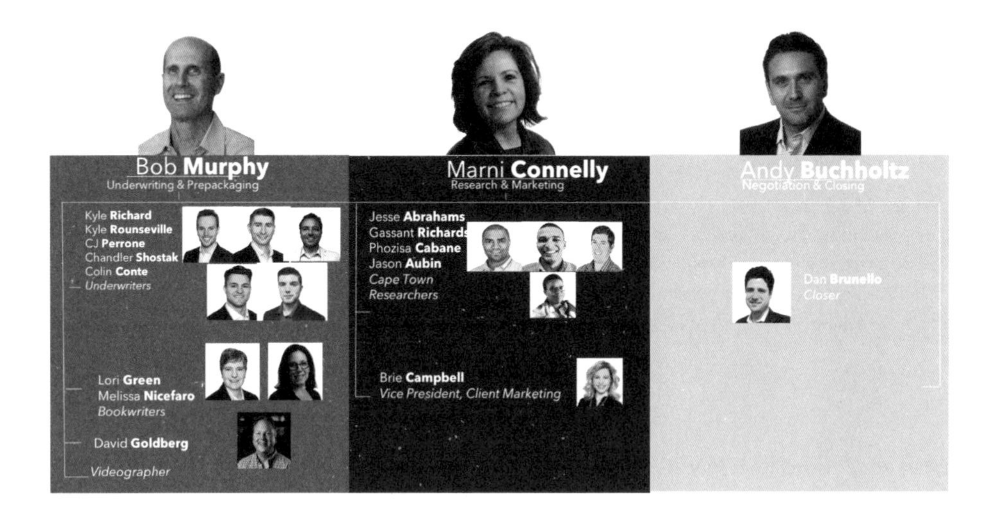

Auction Results

Total # of Buyer Contacts	# of Strategics	# of PEGs	# of Days Launch to Close	# of Books Out	# of Bids	# of LOIs	Buyers who attended Mgt. Meetings	Buyers Submitting LOIs
20,511	14,493	6,018	164	102	11	5	• Mitch Mankosa, Freeport, NY	• Yes
							• PEG, New York, NY	• Yes
							• Strategic, New York, NY	• Yes
							• PEG, Hartford, CT	• Yes
							• PEG, Santa Ana, CA	• No

Transaction Highlights

What were the reasons our client wanted to sell?	The owners, a married couple, had been working day-to-day on the business for many years and now wished to retire.
Main reason our client chose the buyer they closed with	Our clients were pleased that the buyer offered 90% cash at closing and some owner retained equity. Also, as the buyer has a strong military background, he is the ideal person to win new government contracts as a veteran-owned enterprise.
Did our client stay on to run the business?	Yes, transitional roles under consulting agreements for 2-3 months.
Did our client roll equity?	Yes, in the form of synthetic warrants equal to 12% of the company's common equity that can be exercised upon a future exit.
Did our client take back paper?	Yes, 5-year seller's note.
Did we get our client more than they wanted for the business?	Yes, a higher-than-average multiple for companies in this industry.
What were the obstacles that we needed to overcome?	An HR issue, multiple funding sources for the deal, and a hurricane-related bank delay were all challenges that arose along the way. Woodbridge facilitated solutions to these issues and the deal closed in 164 days from launch.

Marketing Associate Advocacy. Brie Campbell, Vice President, Client Marketing, highlighted some of the company's attributes to the book holders and elicited 11 bids. She emphasized the strong commitment the sellers had to their employees, giving them all the resources they needed to excel such as an office closer to their homes and excellent benefits.

Buyer Research Team Analysis. The team covered all bases and went out to the paper and paper product manufacturing, distribution and services industries to find potential buyers that would make sense to target. The research team developed a diverse list of strategic buyer categories shown below.

Jesse **Abrahams**
Gassant **Richards**
Phozisa **Cabane**
Jason **Aubin**
Cape Town Researchers

Paper mills	Paperboard mills	Paperboard containers and boxes
Converted paper and paperboard products, except containers	Packing and crating	Paper and paper products
Office equipment	Industrial supplies	Art goods and supplies
Packaging materials	Packaging and labeling services	Industrial supplies merchant wholesalers
Office supply stores	Office services and supplies	Plastic packaging film and sheet
Paper packaging	Plastic packaging	Packaging products
Packing solutions	Industrial packaging	Shipping supplies
Boxes	Poly bags	Government contractors

Underwriting Overview. "This client had a great attitude and was willing to put in the work to prepare for a buyer diligence process. As part of our prepackaging, our team asked the client to analyze their financial results in ways the client had never done before, such as contribution margin by contract, gross profits by salesperson, etc. We anticipated buyers would want to see this information - and they did! These efforts later paid off in sustained deal momentum, and the seller was prepared for all buyer information requests."

Kyle Rounseville
Underwriting Manager

Book Writer Insight. Melissa Nicefaro wrote the Complete Packaging book and observed, "The company's 28-year history in this business, a vast assortment of products and stable client base made this a strong platform for entering the government supply space. The owners were very responsive and supplied all the information we needed as quickly as they could. They were great to work with."

Melissa Nicefaro
Book Writer

Closer Summary. Dan Brunello closed the deal and reported that "Our competitive process allowed us to drive value from initial bids to LOI. Our client was extremely pleased with the transaction value and, particularly, the large percentage of cash-at-close. Given the buyer's veteran status and what that can do to boost the number of contracts the entity is able to bid on, our client is optimistic about the future of the business and is pleased with the upside potential of his warrants."

Dan Brunello
Closer

Why Our Client Finished Big and Had No Regrets. Our clients were able to move to a consulting role and spend time they never had before engaged with family and other non-business activities. There was great chemistry between seller and buyer. There is likely to be an ongoing business relationship between the sellers and the buyer.